all about the MORAVIANS

HISTORY, BELIEFS, AND PRACTICES OF A WORLDWIDE CHURCH

by Edwin A. Sawyer

7th Printing Revision by Robert E. Sawyer

The Moravian Church in North America
1021 Center Street, Bethlehem, Pennsylvania, 18018
459 South Church Street, Winston-Salem, North Carolina, 27101
www.moravian.org

All About the Moravians
History, Beliefs, and Practices of a Worldwide Church

Edwin A. Sawyer
7th Printing Revision by Robert E. Sawyer

Copyright © 1990, 2000, 2008 by the
Interprovincial Board of Communication
Moravian Church in North America
PO Box 1245
Bethlehem, PA 18016-1245
www.moravian.org
All rights reserved.

Library of Congress
Catalog Card Number: 89-69836
ISBN: 978-1-933571-11-9

Book & Cover design:
Sandy Fay, Laughing Horse Graphics, Doylestown, PA.

Front cover photograph: Tim Gilman ©1990.

Inside photographs by Deanna L. Hollenbach,
Interprovincial Board of Communication,
Moravian Church in North America.

Page 32 photo © 2008 Design Pics.

Page 36 photo by Mother's Best Photography,
Sally Abruzzese, Bethlehem, PA.

Page 55 photo by Bill & Margaret Hoffman.
Provided by the Board of World Mission,
Moravian Church in North America.

Printed in the United States of America.

ALL ABOUT THE MORAVIANS

$\mathcal{I}$NTRODUCTION

This is the story of a Protestant denomination that has celebrated its 550th anniversary! When newcomers to the Moravian Church hear this, they are apt to ask, "Does this mean you began before Martin Luther?" And the answer is, "Yes."

A second question often follows: "Are you a foreign or ethnic group?" The answer is a simple, "No." As a matter of fact, very few Moravian congregations in North America have members with roots in Moravia or Bohemia — both provinces of the Czech Republic.

NAME

The name "Moravian" started out as a nickname in eastern Germany in the 1720s because refugees belonging to the church came from Moravia to the estate of the wealthy Saxon nobleman Count Nicholas von Zinzendorf. It is probably fortunate that the nickname was not "Bohemian," because of other connotations of that word. But since many refugees also came from Bohemia, it might have turned out that way.

Actually the official name is the *Unitas Fratrum*, or Unity of Brethren. This was the original name of the church when it was founded back in 1457 in the Bohemian forests.

ECUMENICAL

The Moravians are not a sect. They number more than three-quarters of a million worldwide and stand in the mainstream of Protestantism. They have been members of the World Council of Churches since its inception. They are also active members of the National Council of Churches of Christ in the USA and participants in Christian Churches Together in the USA. The Northern Province of the North American church is a partner in Churches Uniting in Christ, indicating the intention to keep seeking common ground with the wider Christian church.

Moravians do not proselytize. When new churches are being considered, Moravians look for areas with a growing population but few churches so that duplication of effort is avoided. They have always been primarily interested in serving according to local needs and cooperating with other churches as partners.

WHERE FOUND

In the United States, one is most apt to encounter Moravians in eastern Pennsylvania or Forsyth County, North Carolina. Winston-Salem is the hub in the latter state, while old established congregations in Pennsylvania are found in the area of Bethlehem and Lititz.

Actually, though, the first Moravian settlement in the United States was in Savannah, Georgia, in 1735. This endured for just five years. Only after more than 200 years did the Moravians return to Georgia

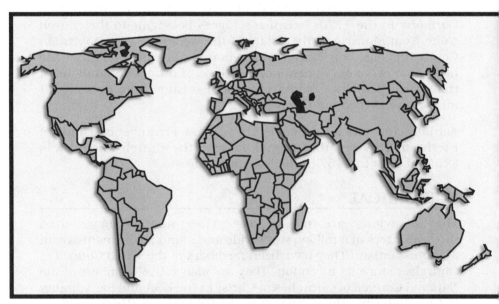

Though statistics are difficult to capture, the Moravian Church in North America has approximately 45,000 members in four provinces: Northern, Southern, Alaska, and Labrador. There are approximately 750,000 Moravians worldwide, with more than two-thirds living in Africa.

— to Stone Mountain, outside of Atlanta. This followed the relatively recent entry of the Moravians into Florida, in Longwood (Orlando), Miami, West Palm Beach, Tampa, Sarasota, and Margate.

Along the eastern seaboard of the United States there are also Moravian churches in New York, New Jersey, Maryland, Virginia, and the District of Columbia. Midwest congregations are in Ohio, Indiana, Michigan, Illinois, Wisconsin, Minnesota, and North Dakota. Since the 1950s churches have developed in Downey and Banning, California.

A cluster of congregations dating back to the late 1800s is found in and around Edmonton and Calgary, Alberta, Canada. More recently, Moravian churches have also been organized in Toronto and Mississauga, Ontario. Among natives of Alaska and Labrador the Moravians have worked for many years. The Alaska province is now independent, while Labrador is emerging steadily from the status of a mission to being self-supporting.

COMPLEXION

For centuries the church "at home," particularly in Europe, has aimed to strengthen a personal relationship with Jesus Christ rather than add to its numbers. This has been accompanied by a vigorous missionary evangelism abroad, especially among people far from the centers of power — people to whom other churches were not ministering.

Of the approximately more than 750,000 Moravians worldwide, only about 60,000, therefore, live in the predominantly white Western world. The remainder are concentrated in Tanzania, South Africa, and the Caribbean.

In the Moravian Archives in Bethlehem, Pennsylvania, there is a very interesting painting called *The First Fruits*. It looks as though it might have been a kind of eighteenth-century United Nations group. Gathered around a representation of Jesus (who almost looks like Count Zinzendorf) are men, women, and children from seventeen different lands. In each case the person is the first convert from his or her tribe or nation. The angels pictured are Germans — the whole painting imaginative and impressive. It reflects the Count's strategy between 1732 and 1760 to gather such first fruits of conversion, as God would see fit to give.

MUSIC

Along with their missionary work, Moravians are well known for their music. In 1501 the Unitas Fratrum published a hymnal in Prague, in the Czech language. When the church came to America, it brought along brass instruments for trombone choirs.

The stately German chorales became the most familiar hymns sung in the Moravian Church, but choirs on the American frontier also sang original anthems written by their pastors and organists. This unusual treasury of sacred music from the late 1700s and early 1800s is celebrated and performed at Moravian Music Festivals in Moravian centers in the United States and Canada — usually every four years.

Music plays an important part in the modern Moravian church as well as in its history. New hymns are written, choirs still sing in multiple harmonies, and bands gather to play at individual congregations and special events. Adding to traditional music, it is not uncommon to find congregations using guitars, drums, keyboards, and steel drums in musical expression.

1

 BRIEF HISTORY

Moravians value their long history. This goes hand in hand with a unique fellowship that is demonstrated by international travel to Moravian centers and visits back and forth within countries where the church is at work. Also, few denominations have regularly convened international meetings such as the Moravian Unity synods, held every seven years.

BEGINNINGS

The church emerged after 1415, when the ashes of the martyr John Hus were scattered along the shores of Lake Constance and flowed on up the Rhine River into northern Europe. Hus was born of humble parents in 1369. The traditional date is July 6. He received his name from the town of his birth, Husinec, an obscure village in southern Bohemia. From his earliest years he breathed the air of political independence and religious liberty.

Bohemia and Moravia were first evangelized in the tenth century by missionaries from Constantinople (Istanbul). These missionaries were priests of the Eastern Orthodox Church and helped make the gospel live for the people by translating parts of the Bible into the native language. As time went by, the Roman Catholic Church pushed northward and eventually gained jurisdiction over the twin countries of Bohemia and Moravia, but the early seeds of love for the Bible were well planted. These countries could not be treated like all the others under Rome.

Encouraged by words and gifts from his friends and neighbors, John Hus entered Charles University in Prague. It was at that time one of the major universities of Europe. There Hus learned philosophy and the arts; but he found his deepest joy in careful study of the Scriptures. He felt, too, that communication with the common people deserved high priority. He could not agree that the Catholic Church of the time, with mass in Latin, was reaching the people.

BETHLEHEM CHAPEL

Hus took his regular degree from the university by 1393 and a master's degree by 1396. Then he was invited to be a lecturer. Within five years he was dean of philosophy. In 1401 he was appointed rector of the entire university. His brilliance was everywhere acknowledged, however, he found his greatest satisfaction in being invited to be the preacher at the Bethlehem Chapel in Prague. He accepted the call and was ordained.

The Bethlehem Chapel had been established a few years before by patriotic Czechs with the stipulation that preaching be in Czech and not Latin. There Hus drew thousands of hearers. The gospel rang out with evangelical fervor. The chapel became a rallying place for seekers of biblical truth, including the royal family. When Rome started getting nervous about the radical ideas expressed, King Wenzel ordered that Hus should be allowed to preach the word of God in peace.

John Hus mural on the wall inside Bethlehem Chapel in Prague

This did not satisfy the church hierarchy. Hus was placed under a ban, forbidding him to preach. He was charged with echoing the ideas of Englishman John Wyclif, called today "the morning star of the Reformation." Wyclif had declared in the previous century that the Bible is the norm of Christian truth. Even the Pope is to be disobeyed if his commands are contrary to Scripture.

As a warning to Hus, over 200 books of Wyclif were burned in the old square in Prague by representatives of Rome. Today a statue of Hus in the same square attests to the city's regard for Hus' independent convictions and defiance of the church hierarchy. A severe power struggle followed. It was enmeshed with the issue of indulgences — the same issue Martin Luther battled a century later. The Pope had messengers all over Europe selling slips of paper guaranteeing the church's forgiveness of sin — at a price.

COUNCIL OF CONSTANCE

The pincers were drawn ever tighter around Hus. He was summoned by the Pope to a council called in Constance, on the Swiss border of Germany. Hus's defense centered on the issues of salvation and the nature of the church. Christ alone is the true Head of the church, he said. Popes through ignorance and the love of money make mistakes. The forgiveness of sin is not a financial transaction but comes from God's grace.

As to church practice, Hus preached that believers have the right to hear the gospel in their own tongue. Communion should be given to the laity in both kinds — the bread and the wine. The Hussite cup thus came to be the symbol of this principle.

All was to no avail — neither Hus's eloquence, logic, sincerity, nor the support of 250 noblemen who protested the prejudiced and summary trial. John Hus was condemned and his body burned at the stake outside Constance, by coincidence on his forty-sixth birthday, July 6, 1415.

Chalice, symbol of early Czech Hussites

Ideas do not die by burning either bodies or books. A Hussite League was formed to preserve the martyr's principles. National independence from the political power of the Holy Roman Empire was the goal. The new king of Bohemia was defied, and with him "all of Europe." It is remarkable that with only native military forces this independence could prevail for sixteen years. Remember that this small nation in this century has been surrounded by often hostile countries: Germany, Austria, Hungary, Poland, and Russia.

WALDENSIAN SUPPORT

On July 22, 1419, a religious rally of 40,000 persons gathered at Mount Tabor in southern Bohemia. They received communion in both kinds (the bread and cup) in defiance of the Roman authorities. High with hopes that in Bohemia would be born both political freedom and a church true to the New Testament, many Waldensians migrated from the valleys of southeastern France and western Italy to join them. These were simple folk who since 1174 and the time of Peter Waldo resisted the papacy and quietly practiced a biblical piety. Their church, never highly organized but still alive today, came to be called "the mother of the Reformation." A generation later the Unitas Fratrum would send

ᗰORAVIANS TODAY

THE LOVEFEAST

The lovefeast service was added to Moravian worship in the Zinzendorf era. It seemed appropriate because the August 13, 1727 revival (when a special outpouring of the Holy Spirit was felt) was accompanied by a feasting on food and the Spirit on the Count's estate. Doctrinal disputes and personal hostilities were laid aside, and a new spirit of love and fellowship prevailed. It brought to mind Acts 2:46, when the early Christians "partook of food with glad and generous hearts." (See also Jude 12)

Today lovefeasts are held with varying frequency across the Moravian Church. In the Midwest they occur only occasionally. In the South a congregation may have three or more on Christmas Eve, another on Good Friday evening, on a church anniversary, a mission occasion, and other days. In the North, in the Eastern District, they may occur on Children's Day, Christian Family Sunday, or during Epiphany.

three men to the Waldensians beyond Bohemia to receive a "pure" ministerial ordination.

The Hussite wars ended in May 1434 with a measure of tolerance granted only to the semi-Protestants, called Utraquists. The more radical Taborite cause was exterminated, but in the small village of Kunwald, about 120 miles east of Prague, a band of Bible-centered brothers and sisters in 1457 formed the Unitas Fratrum, the Unity of Brethren. Their leader, Gregory, pointed them to the writings of Hus and a peace-loving farmer, Peter of Chelcic; and Peter's commentaries on Scripture became the rules of the new church.

Visitors are often impressed with the unique blend of dignity and informality in the service.

Normally there is no sermon, but an address is common on missionary occasions. In the 1700s it was a time for reading letters from missionaries.

The basic structure is singing, alternately by the congregation and choir(s). After an opening hymn and prayer, women sacristans or *dieners* (sometimes dressed in white and wearing a lace cap or haube) pass baskets of sweet buns from row to row of worshipers. Each person holds a bun and beverage (usually coffee) served by the men carrying trays of cups, until all are served.

The unison partaking of the bun and coffee demonstrates the congregation's family spirit and promotes Christian fellowship. There is no sacramental significance to the elements of food, although some persons may look at the bun and be reminded of Christ's feeding of the five thousand.

A possible supplement to the lovefeast is becoming popular in many congregations, namely a fellowship hour after the morning service. Worshipers are invited to stay for coffee and perhaps other refreshment.

The fortunes of the Brethren, after gaining from the Waldensians in 1467 a new line of ministers, free from what they regarded as Catholic corruption, varied according to the resolve of the Roman Church. The cruel Inquisition was always near at hand to oppress nonconformists in Bohemia or wherever. The Brethren established schools. They published the first Protestant hymnal in 1501, as we have noted. The monumental Kralitz Bible was translated from the Greek and Latin into Czech and is still a recognized treasure of Christendom.

GROWTH AND THE COMENIUS ERA

The membership of the Brethren rose steadily to more than 200,000, but as the politics of Bohemia changed and Rome felt its power threatened more and more, martyrdom fell to many.

MORAVIANS TODAY

AT MEAL TIME

Most Protestant denominations encourage family prayers before eating. When it comes to the Moravians, probably the special ingredient of table grace is the desire to have Jesus himself as the unseen guest. The simplest prayer is found in the *Daily Texts*:

> *Come, Lord Jesus, our Guest to be,*
> *And bless these gifts bestowed by thee.*

To this is sometimes added,

> *Bless thy dear ones everywhere;*
> *Keep them in thy love and care. Amen.*

Even more universally used is the blessing that can either be spoken in unison or sung to the tune "Old Hundredth" or a number of other tunes:

> *Be present at our table, Lord;*
> *Be here and everywhere adored*
> *From your all-bounteous hand our food*
> *May we receive with gratitude. Amen.*

The Thirty Years' War broke out in 1618, and at the battle of White Mountain in 1620 the Protestant cause in Bohemia was so completely crushed that the only recourse left to the Brethren was to go underground. They were not as fortunate as Martin Luther and John Calvin, whose reformation was safeguarded by more favorable conditions in Germany and Switzerland.

The abundantly talented Bishop John Amos Comenius was now the leader of the Bohemian Brethren,

John Amos Comenius

In no other frequently used table grace is the evidence of the Moravian heart religion as obvious as in the following. The verses are also used at times in lovefeast odes:

> *Lord, the gifts thou dost bestow*
> *Can refresh and cheer us too;*
> *But no gift can to the heart*
> *Be what thou, our Savior, art.*
>
> *Jesus' mercies never fail:*
> *This we prove at every meal.*
> *Lord, we thank thee for thy grace,*
> *Gladly join to sing thy praise. Amen.*

There is also this blessing, containing lines from a hymn that recalls Christ's eating with two of his friends at Emmaus on the first Easter day (Luke 24:13-32):

> *Be known to us in breaking bread,*
> *But do not then depart;*
> *Savior, abide with us and spread*
> *Your table in our heart. Amen.*

but was forced to flee to Poland, taking with him a small band of refugees. They prayed that God would preserve a "hidden seed" to glorify his name. The seed was indeed preserved, but Comenius's talents had to be used in other areas, from his new home in Poland.

He published *The World in Pictures*, the first illustrated textbook for children. Other scholarly works followed, and Comenius so refashioned education in Poland, Sweden, England, and Transylvania that he has been called the father of modern education. Tradition says that Governor Winthrop of Massachusetts invited him to become president of Harvard University.

But the needs of his underground church claimed his loyal shepherding. Feeling that God had a special plan for the ancient Brethren, Comenius passed on the line of bishops to his son-in-law, who in turn consecrated his son a bishop. This was done with the hope that someday the ancient church would be given rebirth. The rebirth occurred early in the spring of 1722 in Saxony, across the Polish and Bohemian borders of what is now eastern Germany.

RENEWAL

Count Nicholas Ludwig von Zinzendorf was only 22 when the first refugees settled on his family's estate. He was a nobleman born for religion.

Sympathetic toward any who were persecuted for their faith, he allowed first a trickle of Moravians, then a full stream to come. Houses were built, with the village taking on the name of Herrnhut, meaning "The Lord watches over."

For a time Zinzendorf pursued a legal career, which his family charted out for him. His experience of Christ controlled him, however, and led him to see his calling as an agent for the renewal of the Unitas Fratrum. This he accomplished while qualifying for ordination as a Lutheran pastor. Indeed, he lived and died within the Lutheran state church.

As for the vigorously renewed Moravian Church, centered on his estate, he thought it might endure for "perhaps fifty years." In that time the Brethren could be used, he felt, as the spiritual leaven for the renewal of all of Christendom. It was a grand scheme, with Zinzendorf seeing no inconsistency in his remaining in the state church and still being a bishop of the Unity, to which office he was elected.

The count said, "I have but one passion, and that is He (Jesus), only He." To guide others in a like experience of the religion of the heart, Herrnhut was divided into small groups, of like people, or choirs, for prayer, Bible study, and spiritual sharing. The result was a Moravian Pentecost on August 13, 1727. Among the results was establishment of Moravian centers in other parts of Germany, England, Denmark, Holland, Switzerland, Sweden, and America.

But unquestionably the revival blossomed into fullest flower in the dispatching of fully 200 missionaries to all the continents by the time of the count's death in 1760. Without Zinzendorf's charismatic leadership, his breathtaking vision, and the committing of all his financial wealth, the Moravian Church would not have been revived.

Count Nicholas Ludwig von Zinzendorf

2

THE MORAVIAN INFLUENCE IN NORTH AMERICA

To get the feel of how the Moravians began and continue in two American centers, one should spend a day walking the streets of the historic districts of Winston Salem, North Carolina and Bethlehem, Pennsylvania. There you will see the stately, durable buildings in brick or stone that look like a scene from eighteenth-century Germany. A walk through the carefully restored gardens or a pause in the venerable places of worship will give you a sense of peace and composure, which Moravians always treasure.

The same inspiration may come to you in Lititz or Nazareth, Pennsylvania, and Bethabara, North Carolina, where more modest restoration has taken place and tourism is not so obvious. The museums show the artifacts of an early era, and the exhibit buildings remind of the contributions of the tanners, the millers, the weavers, the potters, the tailors, the gunsmiths, the bakers, and a dozen others. In New Philadelphia, Ohio, a professional cast portrays the success and tragedy of another historic time — that of the Indian missions in Ohio — in the outdoor drama "Trumpet in the Land."

Moravians had a unity of purpose in the 1700s, even as they try to sustain one today. As a minority culture, they gave up unique dress as well as the idea of closed communities over 150 years ago, but a simple lifestyle is still commended. Few Moravians are known for their wealth.

The vocations they follow today are apt to be teaching, clerking, law, medicine, small business, farming, and labor. Ideally, they try to live "a quiet and peaceable life in all godliness and honesty," trusting that they find acceptance by the Savior who has led them safely through so many centuries of change and adventure.

EARLY SETTLEMENTS

When the first band of Moravian settlers arrived on General Oglethorpe's land in Savannah, Georgia, in 1735, they had several motives. Missions among the slaves on St. Thomas had been started three years earlier. The church believed that Native Americans should be offered the gospel too.

The New World intrigued Count Zinzendorf and his associates. It could be a haven for the Moravians who lived under a cloud of suspicion in the Old World. Were there not thousands of white settlers who would respond to the gospel as the Moravians interpreted it?

Unfortunately, after five years of poor crops, fever from living in infectious lowlands, and the threat of being drafted for military service against the Spanish in Florida, the small group of pioneers gave up the Savannah effort and set out for Pennsylvania.

George Whitefield, a friend of John and Charles Wesley and an eloquent evangelist, needed carpenters and craftsmen to build a home and school for African children he hoped to bring from South Carolina. Whitefield knew what a powerful influence a group of Moravians had on John Wesley while the group crossed the Atlantic. He learned later of Aldersgate, England, where Wesley felt the oft-told "strange warming of the heart," and of his conversations with Moravian pastor Peter Boehler.

Would not half a dozen faithful brethren be just the right builders for Whitefield near the "forks of the Delaware," in Pennsylvania, in the settlement later named Nazareth? Whitefield offered them employment; they accepted. Before the gray stone building, still known as the Whitefield House, in Nazareth was completed, doctrinal disputes led the evangelist to discharge the Moravians. Fortunately the brethren were offered 500 acres of land by William Allen along the Lehigh River, nine miles south of Nazareth. Soon afterward Whitefield abandoned his project and sold the property to the Moravians. The barony of Nazareth, so-called, became a prosperous community and the breadbasket of the Pennsylvania Moravian settlements.

BETHLEHEM AND LITITZ

Count Zinzendorf visited the new community along the Lehigh in 1741 and confirmed its biblical name, Bethlehem. On Christmas Eve, in surroundings of very simple living quarters, with the primitive community's animals nearby, it occurred to the count that

**Central Moravian Church,
Bethlehem, PA**

*Not Jerusalem,
Lowly Bethlehem
Twas that gave us Christ
to save us,
Not Jerusalem.*

The romance and the frontier struggle of Bethlehem form a story well told elsewhere. So is that of Lititz, founded in Lancaster County, Pennsylvania, in 1754 and named for a town in Moravia. The goal in both these towns was to establish communities free from adverse outside influences and to support the carrying of the gospel wherever the Savior called. The idea of keeping the settlements closed to outsiders was to give way a century later. The magnificent stone buildings on Bethlehem's Church Street and the majestic Central Church, completed in 1806, attest to the seriousness of Moravian purpose and the competence of those early community planners.

Today there are six Moravian congregations in the Bethlehem limits, with a membership of about 3,300. The Northern Province headquarters of the denomination is also housed in a building in Bethlehem, Pennsylvania, genuine evidence of Moravian culture lingers. The "heart religion" is probably more restrained than of old, but the good common sense of church members and their spirit of cooperation and solid citizenship attract both admirers and new adherents.

The same is true in Lititz, where the Moravian Church and Linden Hall School for Girls dominate the church square. Here is the second largest congregation in the Northern Province, with over 900 total members. In Central Pennsylvania also are located the older Lebanon, Lancaster, and York congregations along with two newer congregations.

Closer to Bethlehem are Nazareth, Emmaus, and a dozen other congregations organized since the colonial period. One can visit the Brethren's House both in Lititz and Bethlehem where bronze tablets recall the use of the buildings as hospitals for Revolutionary soldiers. Both Benjamin Franklin and George Washington made visits to Bethlehem.

METROPOLITAN NEW YORK

Count Zinzendorf and his associates were quite conscious of the strategic importance of New York and Philadelphia. Only one Moravian church has survived in Philadelphia, while the First Church of Manhattan, founded in 1748, now ministers primarily to Moravians from the Caribbean in its regular program.

However, half a mile from the church is a denomination-sponsored residence for formerly homeless people known as the Moravian Open Door. Forty persons are housed and rehabilitated, with church support.

Staten Island, across the New York harbor, witnessed the founding of a Moravian Church at New Dorp in 1763, followed by three other congregations still ministering on the island. In the other boroughs of New York City there are an additional five congregations, many of whose members are first- or second-generation immigrants from the Caribbean.

The steady influx of Caribbean Moravians to both Canada and the United States has opened up a new ministry beyond New York as well: in Toronto and Mississauga, Ontario, Canada; Miami, Florida; and Washington, D.C. Nicaraguan Moravians have formed groups in Texas and California. Good race relationships constantly need cultivating, but the Moravian Church by nature of its long outreach to the Third World has consistently fostered cooperation and harmony wherever it works.

As early as the 1740s the Moravians convened the so-called Pennsylvania Synods as evidence of their ecumenical spirit (initiatives aimed at greater religious unity or cooperation). These brought together representatives of many denominations (working mostly among German settlers) for mutual inspiration and common planning. Because they were probably ahead of their time, they did not endure.

The balance of the Eastern District of the church embraces a congregation in Union, New Jersey, and three in southern New Jersey; four in Maryland and the District of Columbia; and eight in Ohio — all but two in Tuscarawas County, with the two newest near Columbus.

A significant center for members of the Eastern District for over 50 years has been the Hope Conference and Renewal Center, available for year-round camping and conference use in northwestern New Jersey.

MORAVIANS TODAY

IN EDUCATION

As heirs of Bishop John Amos Comenius (1592-1670), Moravians have always been dedicated to education. They were among the first in America to take the education of women seriously. A seminary for girls was begun in Bethlehem, Pennsylvania, in 1742 (following a preliminary year in Germantown, Pennsylvania). Linden Hall in Lititz, Pennsylvania, followed in 1746 and Salem Academy in Winston-Salem, North Carolina, in 1772. Many non-Moravians, as well as Moravians, have received their education in these schools.

A boys' school in early Bethlehem, with the seminary for girls, led to the present Moravian Academy, a coeducational day school for kindergarten through high school. Present enrollment is well over 800, divided into lower school, middle school, and upper school.

To Salem Academy has been added Salem College, with a broad liberal arts program and a school of music. Linden Hall is a boarding school for girls of middle school and high school age. A few day students are admitted.

The need for trained ministry led to the establishment of Moravian Theological Seminary in 1807. This fine institution fostered the parallel establishment of Moravian College. Numerically the coeducational college now far eclipses the Seminary; but their campuses are adjacent in Bethlehem, and the administration and some facilities are shared. National

VARYING EMPHASES

While it can be truly said that the Moravian Church influences other groups of Christians out of proportion to its numbers, it is also true that the church is considerably influenced by the milieu of the areas where it works. In the South it tends to be more evangelistic than in the North.

Moravian Theological Seminary, Bethlehem, PA

magazines have ranked Moravian among the best small colleges in America.

The theological seminary is unique in that it serves the whole Moravian Unity. Ministerial students from England, Germany, Tanzania, and the Caribbean frequently find their way to Bethlehem for special study.

The newest partner in education is the Teofilo Kisangi University in Mbeya, Tanzania. Theological education for pastors is just one of several programs offered by the University.

In addition, the Moravian churches of the eastern Caribbean hold a chair of theology at the ecumenical United Theological College of the West Indies in Kingston, Jamaica. Other Moravian institutions for the training of ministers are found in Alaska, Honduras, Suriname, and Southern Africa.

The ministry of the church to Germans in southern New Jersey and in Alberta (Canada), Wisconsin, North Dakota, and Minnesota (in the late nineteenth and early twentieth centuries) made liturgy readily acceptable. It also influenced Western District Moravian architecture. The same sort of influence came to a degree from the small number of Wisconsin churches consisting primarily of Scandinavians.

$\mathcal{M}$ORAVIANS TODAY

CHRISTMAS EVE AND YEAR'S END

Reference has been made elsewhere in this book to Christmas customs of the Moravians: building a putz, distributing beeswax candles, hanging a multi-pointed star. The lighted star, symbolizing Christ as the Light of the world, has a special beauty as it hangs in a church or in the hallway of a home, or on the front porch.

Who invented the Advent or Christmas star is not known. It seems to have originated around 1850 in a Moravian school in Niesky, Germany. Evening handicraft sessions at the school produced a few stars, but in the 1880s a student at Niesky, Pieter Verbeek, made stars for sale. His son Harry later set up a star factory in Herrnhut, Germany.

From there the custom spread to America, along with wider star production and use. In Edmonton, Alberta, Canada, a star makers' group earned thousands of dollars for missions by producing various sizes, designs, and colors of plastic stars.

The beeswax candle is trimmed before Christmas with a red or white fireproof fluffy paper skirt. This in a practical sense helps to catch the rapidly melting candle wax, while the color

Normally Moravian church interiors are quite plain — no altar, a central pulpit with open Bible, possibly a lectern to the side, and a freestanding communion table. In Ohio, Methodists and Moravians share much in architecture and practice; in Canada pluralism exerts an influence; in California, people's uprootedness leads to easy acceptance of many patterns.

of the paper reminds worshipers of the purity and sacrificial gift of Christ.

Each worshiper receives a lighted candle, from sacristans or dieners moving quietly through the nave on Christmas Eve. The aesthetic effect of a darkened church with hundreds of softly glowing candles lighting up the faces of young and old and proclaiming Christ as the Light of the world is unforgettable.

At this point of the Christmas Eve vigil service a child sings the traditional Moravian hymn "Morning Star." After two solo lines by the child, the congregation responds with the same lines, and all join in a final unison line.

Only a few Moravian Churches in North America continue to hold Watch Night services on New Year's Eve, but it remains a very popular service among Moravians of a Caribbean and Central American background. The tradition is for the minister to keep preaching until interrupted by a trombone choir or brass and reed band, right at the stroke of midnight. Christ could return, so the symbolism of interruption goes, at any time — unexpectedly. The horns proclaim a new year with the chorale "Now Thank We All Our God."

The minister then joins with the congregation in singing — the sermon unfinished. An earlier custom of reading memorabilia of the chief events of the passing year has not survived.

In Indiana and southern Illinois there is a tinge of the Bible-belt approach to religion. Many of the churches in Florida have a distinctively Caribbean style.

WESTERN DISTRICT

The Western District of the Northern Province of the Moravian Church comprises some 34 congregations in six Midwestern states and California. District headquarters is located in Sun Prairie, a suburb of Madison, Wisconsin.

The Mt. Morris Moravian Camp and Conference Center, near Wautoma, Wisconsin, and the extensive Marquardt Village in Watertown, Wisconsin, a full service senior living (older adult) community, take their places with the Sun Prairie headquarters in helping to bind Moravians in the district to each other. In addition, the senior high and college age youth camp, Chetek, has fostered ties that help forge district purpose and denominational participation.

Sturgeon Bay Moravian Church, located in Door County, WI.

The 18 Wisconsin churches are scattered across the state from Madison to Door County in the far north. Large congregations serve the cities of Green Bay, Sturgeon Bay, Wisconsin Rapids, Watertown, and Lake Mills (the third largest church of the Northern Province). Most other congregations are rural, although some of them are taking on more and more of a suburban character.

A church in Daggett is on the Michigan side of Green Bay. The other Michigan churches include Unionville, near Saginaw Bay, and one in the Detroit suburbs. West Salem, Illinois, and Hope, Indiana are also home to Moravian congregations.

The Minnesota churches are to the west and south of Minneapolis and are seven in number. Auburn Manor and Talheim in Chaska are relatively new homes for older adults. In North Dakota there is a congregation in Fargo, with three others in rural Cass County, to the west. The District is rounded out with two churches in California, one in Banning and another in Downey.

SOUTHERN PROVINCE

In terms of expansion by the church in North Carolina, the late 1800s and the first half of the twentieth century were particularly vigorous. Salem, Bethabara, Bethania, Friedland, Hope, and Friedberg — all from the 1700s — are the oldest among 25 congregations in Winston-Salem. The newest, Cordero de Dios (Lamb of God), serves a rapidly growing Latino population and continues a long ministry in the neighborhood previously served by Immanuel Moravian Church. In the last five decades new churches were started in Florida, near Atlanta, Georgia, and in all five major metropolitan areas of North Carolina.

Home Moravian Church, Winston-Salem, NC

For Southern Moravians, young and old, the Laurel Ridge Camp, Conference, and Retreat Center provides year-round inspiration and Christian education most notably through its camping programs. In 2007, an extensive building campaign added a large facility for conference use to Moravians and non-Moravians. It is located near the Blue Ridge Parkway, approximately 70 miles northwest of Winston-Salem, North Carolina.

The Moravian Music Foundation, based in Winston-Salem, has done much to publicize the church through preserving, sharing, and celebrating the musical culture of Moravians. Scores of churches of other denominations have come to appreciate and use the sincere, melodic choral and instrumental music written primarily between 1760 and 1810.

The composers were pastors, organists, and choirmasters who came to this country from Europe. The simplicity and beauty of both text and composition reflect the faith and versatility of a body of believers whom Zinzendorf liked to call "God's happy people." All was written with a characteristically sublime devotion to Jesus Christ.

SOCIAL CONSCIOUSNESS

Today the needs of older adults are being met by Moravians through retirement communities in Winston-Salem, North Carolina; Watertown, Wisconsin; Chaska, Minnesota; and Nazareth, Bethlehem, and Lititz, Pennsylvania. Most provide a wide range of residential opportunities from cottages to apartments to skilled nursing care.

Moravians provide the above-mentioned services of health and education in Christ's name, and peacemaking has often been part of the Moravian witness. The church has long emphasized ministry with the marginalized, but it is not usually prominent in the arena of public advocacy. Many do run for local and county office. The last Moravian representative in Congress served in the 1940s, but Moravian judges are sitting on the bench in several states.

Members take the voting franchise very seriously. Causes such as world peace, protection of the environment, housing for the homeless, women's rights, health care, race relations, and the relief of poverty are served in full proportion by Moravians. Synods of the church regularly discuss these issues and plan action. For three decades the Sunnyside Ministry has served low-income residents on the south side of Winston-Salem, North Carolina. The Moravian Open Door in New York provides housing and supportive services to New York's homeless, distressed, and underserved older population.

It is also a church that likes to remember Benjamin LaTrobe, one of the early architects of the national Capitol in Washington. He was a Moravian, as are singer George Hamilton IV, and Bobby Thomson, whose 1950 baseball home run "was heard around the world." Television star Andy Griffith once played in the Mt. Airy, North Carolina, Moravian Easter band; and the late astronaut Donald Eiseley was married to a Moravian from Gnadenhutten, Ohio.

3

WHAT MORAVIANS BELIEVE

Moravians have no strange or unusual beliefs. As mentioned earlier, the denomination is not a confessional church in the sense that it has written a formal creed like the Augsburg Confession of the Lutheran Church or the Westminster Confession of the Presbyterians. Nevertheless, doctrinal outlines have been written, such as *The Ground of the Unity* and *Essential Features of the Unity* (1995).

Here it is clear that modern Moravians are still true children of Zinzendorf in their Christ-centeredness. *The Ground of the Unity* says in an opening paragraph:

> *With the whole of Christendom we share faith in God the Father, the Son, and the Holy Spirit. We believe and confess that God has revealed himself once and for all in his Son Jesus Christ; that our Lord has redeemed us with the whole of humanity by his death and resurrection; and that there is no salvation apart from him. We believe that he is present with us in the Word and the Sacrament; that he directs and unites us through his Spirit and thus forms us into a church.*

Moravians are also consistent in their continued emphasis on heart religion:

> *The belief of the Church is effected and preserved through the testimony of Jesus Christ and through the work of the Holy Spirit. This testimony calls each individual personally, and leads each one to the recognition of sin and to the acceptance of the redemption achieved by Christ. In fellowship with Him the love of Christ becomes more and more the power of the new life, power which penetrates and shapes the entire person. As God's Spirit so affects living belief in the hearts of the individuals, He grants them the privilege to share in the fruits of Christ's salvation and membership in His body. — The Ground Of The Unity, 1995*

THE BIBLE

Moravians are Bible believers, but not in the literal sense. They believe that certain Bible chapters like Genesis 1 are to be understood symbolically and not literally. The same would be true with regard to some of Jesus' parables and his tendency to use hyperbole.

Numerical and linguistic errors have crept into the long journey of the original Hebrew and Greek texts through endless copying and translation. Nevertheless, dynamically in its total message, Scripture is reliable. It provides the essentials of belief. Hence *The Ground of the Unity* asserts: "The Triune God as revealed in the Holy Scriptures of the Old and New Testament is the only source of our life and salvation; and this Scripture is the sole standard of the doctrine and faith of the Unitas Fratrum and therefore shapes our life."

This means that when doctrinal and ethical issues arise, Moravians ask first: "Does the Bible speak directly to this?" If the answer is yes, the message of Scripture is the official position of the church. The Ten Commandments are non-debatable absolutes because they have stood the test in many civilizations and are clearly outlined in both Exodus and Deuteronomy in the Old Testament.

The Lord's Prayer is the ultimate prayer because Jesus uttered it, and it is recorded in Matthew and Luke of the New Testament. The Apostles' Creed passes muster as a third basic element in every catechism because it is a simplified summary of New Testament doctrine and the teaching of the early church.

BASICS AND "ESSENTIALS"

The Moravian Church maintains that all creeds formulated by the Christian Church stand in need of constant testing in the light of Holy Scripture. Nevertheless, its members frequently ask for interpretation of the word essentials in the so-called motto of the church (see pages 70-71).

One way of satisfying this request is to call attention to a statement of cardinal truths of doctrine made by a Unity Synod more than 100 years ago. Bishop Kenneth Hamilton in his *History of the Moravian Church* (p. 319) states: "Since 1879 Moravians have accepted eight truths as fundamental to the faith." While not regarded by every Moravian as "essential," these eight doctrines are all biblical and follow the one fixed essential: *To become a C...* *one needs to accept Jesus Christ as Savior and Lord.* Thi... starting point of the faith journey; and God's grace can be c... on to help the individual grow in Christian service, witnes... enlightenment.

The eight cardinal or basic truths are:

1. The universal depravity (sinful tendency) of human nature. Moravians do not dwell on this morbidly but believe that history all too clearly gives repeated evidence of this truth.

2. God's love shown in his choosing us to be his. Ephesians 1:4 says that even before the world was created, a divine plan was at work for humanity, to reach out and draw us to Christ.

3. The real godhead and the real humanity of Jesus. Here is a mystery debated for centuries with the last word still to be spoken. Jesus took on himself human flesh that he might be like his brothers and sisters in all things, yet without sin.

4. Reconciliation with God. People are not by nature righteous but must be put right through the sacrificial love (cross) of Christ.

5. The doctrine of the Holy Spirit. God within us points out our sin; leads us to Christ; by grace shows us the truth; guides us to faith; and gives us assurance that we are his children.

6. Good works. These are fruit of the Spirit. They identify the Christian as a person who by faith is given power to follow God's commands gratefully, willingly, and lovingly.

7. The fellowship of believers. They are all one in Jesus Christ, the Head of his Body. Through him all are members one of another.

8. The second coming of the Lord in glory. The dead will be raised with a new body, and unbelievers will be judged.

Volumes have been written about heaven, the afterlife, and the second coming. Moravians recognize the prophecies of Daniel and Revelation on these subjects. They are aware of coming events described in Matthew 24 and 25 (and parallels in Mark and Luke) but regard the fine details as too veiled to allow elaborate dogma. Is it not enough to enjoy Christ's words, "Because I live, you shall live also" (John 14:19), and leave it at that?

OTHER CONSIDERATIONS

To many Moravians, significant points of belief come most clearly to the forefront in the worship observances of Christmas, Holy Week, and Easter. To put it theologically, Moravian doctrine centers in the advent, passion (suffering), and resurrection of Jesus.

Late in November or early in December, depending on when the season of Advent begins, Moravians hang multi-pointed stars in their homes and churches to proclaim that "the Light has come." A

$\mathcal{M}$ORAVIANS TODAY

IN PRAYER

Moravians share with other Christians the conviction that prayer is very important. An effort is made every Sunday to try to give appropriate expression to public prayer. During the week many small groups of Moravians meet for prayer.

In the 1980s a simple publication, *Onward*, was started in the Southern Province of the U.S. Originally, just a single sheet issued monthly, now a multi-paged document, it has a circulation of 17,000 copies. It suggests a person or cause (on the mission or world scene) to pray for each day. A modern version of the publication is available online.

Much older than the modern prayer practices is the remarkable Hourly Intercession. This was the "prayer meeting that lasted 100 years." When missionaries began to leave the putz or crèche in homes or churches may be constructed to give children and adults the reminder that simple historic events surround God's coming to earth in human form.

Cantatas, anthems, orchestral accompaniments, bell ringing — all proclaim the joy of the event. And by the time Christmas Eve rolls around, beeswax candles by the thousands are lighted in Moravian churches. The good news is that salvation in Christ is offered to all, to dispel every element of darkness.

EASTERTIDE

In Lent and Holy Week a different mood and message prevail. Out of love the Savior suffered humiliation and death. This calls for a period of serious reflection and penitence. Lenten services are held

---

Moravian center of Herrnhut for remote and dangerous places in the 1700s, those who remained at home agreed to pray for the missionaries around the clock. Every hour of every day some member of the church in Herrnhut or elsewhere was praying for the gospel messengers.

Time caused this practice to disappear. But when the denomination approached its 500th anniversary celebration in 1957, it was agreed by the international church that the Hourly Intercession should be revived. In North America it is known as the Unity Prayer Watch.

Year after year now, each of the provinces of the church worldwide takes a block of time. It is responsible to divide out its share of days or weeks among its congregations. After that, local members or families volunteer to cover a half or full hour sometime in the day or night to be in prayer for the stated needs of the church.

Characteristically the denominational leadership submits devotional guidelines and lists of subjects for prayer. Thus a chain of prayer is sustained. Devoted members become part of a corporate experience across national and geographical lines; and remarkable spiritual growth is reported.

in this mood. Then, on Palm Sunday Christ's triumphal entry into Jerusalem is celebrated with the singing of a rousing antiphonal hymn, "Hosanna."

On that evening or on Monday evening the mood of quiet reflection settles in as most churches begin reading from a little book, *Readings for Holy Week.* It contains a rehearsal, in the words of the four Gospels, of the teachings and acts of Jesus in the last week on earth before his death.

Interspersed in the biblical narrative are hymns in the solemn strains of the Bach-like chorale.

Messages like "My Savior was betrayed" penetrate deeply into the soul as the choir or congregation sings. By Good Friday afternoon, when the seven words from the cross are read, teary eyes are common. The reality of Christ's sacrifice is overwhelming; and the message of "Love Divine, All Loves Excelling," has reached many a heart.

In many congregations Friday evening brings a quiet, meditative hour in lovefeast, with reflection on human mortality. Then Moravians are ready for the triumphant experience of Easter. On graveyards decorated with resurrection flowers, or in churches scented with banks of lilies, a special Easter morning liturgy is recited — often called the essence of Moravian belief. It reviews the common faith of all Christians. After each paragraph spoken by the leader comes the fitting reply: "This we truly believe."

A pamphlet written in this century by two Moravian bishops, one in England and one in the United States, is entitled "The Spirit of the Moravian Church." The principles enunciated serve well to characterize Moravians in their mode of worship, and to place specific doctrines in perspective:

- Moravians emphasize simplicity.

- Their piety reflects happiness rather than dour discipline.

- They are un-intrusive (or unobtrusive), respecting the rights and feelings of others.

- They perceive Christian fellowship as a gift of Christ. It is rooted in a common devotion to the Lord and grows through heart-to-heart conversation and experience.

- Christian service is perceived as a mind-set. Christians are saved to serve. Therefore the narrow idea of just seeing that "one saves her or his own soul" is insufficient. The mind of the servant urges one on, feeling that no giving of self is enough to match God's love as shown in Jesus Christ.

FAITH EXPRESSED IN WORSHIP

Furthermore, Moravian worship has a spirit of its own. Moravians are not a fully liturgical church as are Catholics, Episcopalians, and Lutherans. The church year is followed through Advent, Christmas, Epiphany, Lent, Easter, Ascension Day, Pentecost, and Trinity. For each of these seasons there is a liturgy, with lofty, devotional use of Scripture intermingled with choir chants and hymns by the congregation.

Communion is normally served to the communicants at their pews, and here too the hymns sung follow a seasonal and doctrinal theme. Then especially during the long Pentecost season, additional liturgies are provided on themes like Intercessions in Time of Crisis, Christian Homes, Christian Unity, Education, Evangelism, National Occasions, Peace and Justice, and Stewardship.

To many, the highest worship experience comes in the praying of the so-called "long" Litany. This is a very complete and uplifting liturgical form with roots in early Christianity. Other fine pieces are the Te Deum Laudamus and a festival doxology. While Moravians treasure a unique tradition of liturgy and hymns, they have always been open to new worship forms that enhance the worship experience of the local congregation. Many churches today use praise music and other contemporary forms.

Emphasizing again the religion of the heart, Moravians feel that the end result of worship should be to lift worshipers into the presence of Christ. Since all liturgies and forms of worship can become sterile and perfunctory, a Unity Synod early in this century declared:

> *All liturgies and litanies should exemplify the spirit of the living church of Christ. The essence and soul of our meetings is not to be found in any (fixed) form, beautiful and attractive as that should ever be, but rather in the religion of the heart.*

MORAVIANS TODAY

BAPTISM, CONFIRMATION, FUNERALS

Like most Protestants, Moravians recognize two sacraments: baptism and the Lord's Supper or Holy Communion. Normally a child of Moravian parents is brought to the church for baptism before the age of six months. The method of baptism is sprinkling or pouring.

In some congregations a sacristan or *diener* (usually a woman dressed in white) brings the child into the service to symbolize the whole congregation's support of the parents, and its acceptance of the child. Two or more sponsors join the parents of the child as supporting believers and friends.

Moravian ministers wear a plain white gown, the surplice, to emphasize the sacredness of baptism, weddings, Holy Communion, and confirmation, and the officiating bishop at ordinations. Since its beginning in 1457, the tendency of the Moravian Church has been toward simplicity; hence a plain white gown with gathered yoke and simple white cloth belt. A few pastors wear a black or other pulpit gown for preaching; but this is not common practice.

Like other Protestants, Moravians believe in the priesthood of all believers. Every Christian has direct access to God. No priest is needed to raise up prayers for the people, as though their own praise and intercession were inadequate. No intermediary is necessary for hearing confession of sins, and the thought of a hierarchy or a centering of power in either clergy or laypersons is unacceptable. Christ is the Head of the church, and the emphasis on religion of the heart accompanies this doctrine.

Children not baptized as infants are baptized when they reach "the age of discretion." Those of like age who were baptized as infants confirm their faith in the rite of confirmation. These services ordinarily are held on Palm Sunday or Pentecost, following a period of careful instruction in Christian doctrine and the practices of the church, and a time of reflection on one's personal relationship with the Lord.

At Moravian funerals in North America it is customary to read a memoir, following the burial liturgy and appropriate Scripture passages. The memoir reviews the life of the deceased, with particular attention given to his or her spiritual pilgrimage. A eulogy as such is discouraged, in accordance with the Moravian concept of simplicity.

One of Zinzendorf's best-known hymns is still included at the graveside service:

> *The Savior's blood and righteousness*
> *My beauty is, my glorious dress;*
> *Thus well arrayed, I need not fear*
> *When in his presence I appear.*

The use of brass instruments at funerals is less common today than formerly, although the note of victory for the faithful in death is still inherent in the Moravian outlook. As for cremation, the church has no objection to its practice; it is becoming more common in most localities.

THE WORLD AROUND US

Over the years, Moravians have been classified as Pietists. Zinzendorf was brought up in Pietist circles and had many friends among them. But his intimate friend and "first lieutenant," Bishop A. G. Spangenberg, tried to make a distinction:

> *There is a difference between a genuine Pietist and a genuine Moravian. The Pietist has his sin in the foreground, [is apt to dwell on it] and looks at the wounds of Jesus; the Moravian has the wounds in the foreground [thus celebrating forgiveness] and looks from them upon his sin [and lays it aside]. The Pietist in his timidity is comforted by the wounds; the Moravian in his happiness is shamed by his sin.*

In today's world also, the notion of being pious might tend to make people forget everyone around them and engage in a kind of exaggerated introspection. Not so, according to *The Ground of the Unity*. The whole world is to be served, for only then does piety find its complete expression.

A WORLD IN NEED

All Christians have an obligation to serve the world in its need.

> *The Moravian Church is a living church with a mission relevant to the everyday life of all humanity. Therefore the Church will, and must, meet the demands made upon it by society as a whole by ministering to the spiritual, social, physical, and economic needs of humanity. This total ministry will express itself in the preaching of the Word, the healing of the sick, the education of both the young and adults to fit them to face life in a competitive society, and by social service to the needy in mind and body. (From the Unity Synod, 1995)*

Concern for the world is not unique to Moravians, but it vigorously calls contemporary members of the church to specific ministries to human need, wherever they arise. The 550th anniversary celebrations in 2007 placed renewed emphasis on this essential commitment to mission outreach.

4

Ⓜ️ORAVIANS IN MANY LANDS

The Moravians are spread out across five continents and about 30 jurisdictional provinces and mission areas. Most of this has resulted from missionary work, begun over 275 years ago. But there are links being strengthened today that keep members of the church feeling closer together than perhaps ever before.

Unity Synods meet every seven years. Representation at these gatherings is the same for each independent province, regardless of size or culture. From their sessions it is determined what shall become joint Unity undertakings, such as the support of a training center for physically and mentally handicapped children and youth in Palestine.

Or special aid may be determined for a school for children of Tibetan refugees in North India. For years the denomination has operated a unique mission along the Tibetan border "on the top of the world." This led to the conversion of several families in the Ladakh area, and their persistence in the Christian faith is a glorious story.

The fruit from this devotion is schools at Assam, Rajpur, Leh, and Khalatse. A carpet-weaving project helps to provide income for the total Moravian witness in North India. More recently a congregation was established in Kathmandu, Nepal. This

Moravian Church, Herrnhut, Germany

39

congregation has birthed two new faith communities and sponsors an active school of worship and music.

NEW TIES FORMED

A solidifying influence for the international Moravian fellowship is love for travel. "Why not visit Moravian centers abroad?" For a generation or more, tours for church members have been organized to the Caribbean, to German and Czech Moravian centers, and to Alaska.

The Internet provides another tool for strengthening ties. An international listserve facilitates exchange of information and opinion on a wide range of topics. Following a youth convocation in Jamaica, a youth steering committee from four continents used email to plan further events, including a Unity-wide call to prayer. Partnerships between congregations oceans apart flourish.

Nearly every year there is a North American Moravian Music Festival, a women's conference, a youth convocation, band festival, or other event. Visiting Moravians from abroad are often in attendance, with lifelong friendships formed. The same holds true with foreign students attending Moravian colleges, the academies, or the Moravian Theological Seminary.

When a missionary society is holding a rally or lovefeast, it is now possible to hear a speaker from Central America, the Caribbean, Africa, Labrador, or Alaska. Years ago the speaker would have been an American missionary who was home on furlough. Then the missionary would tell of the grace of God working to convert an Eskimo or a Miskitu Indian. Today a Yup'ik or Inuit may preach to longtime Moravians in the United States or Canada, urging a fuller commitment to Jesus Christ.

Increasingly, provinces are sharing leadership with each other according to needs and gifts. Two Tanzanian pastors have served in Jamaica, and two married couples from South Africa have spent time in Germany as fraternal workers. Pastors from both Costa Rica and Suriname have taught at the university in Mbeya, Tanzania.

Dozens of Moravians from the North American provinces volunteer for two weeks, a month, or longer to help erect a clinic in Ahuas, Honduras, or a theological training school building for native workers in Bethel, Alaska. Others serve in Christian education and health care.

FOUR PROVINCES
IN THE UNITED STATES AND CANADA

Nine of the Moravian provinces are on or near the North American continent. As indicated earlier, there is a North American Province, North, based in Bethlehem, Pennsylvania, and a North American Province, South, based in Winston-Salem, North Carolina. Some American denominations split at the time of the Civil War. In the Moravian Church two centers developed from the beginning, largely for reasons of communication, especially with Germany.

The two provinces plan and carry out many programs jointly, such as women's work, publications, Christian education, theological education, world mission outreach, a music foundation, a ministries foundation, youth and ministers' convocations, and others. In general the two provinces join together for representation in ecumenical involvements. The Alaska Province is also a partner in the Board of World Mission. Labrador Moravians, who number just over 2300, live and serve in a context of extremely high alcoholism and suicide rates. They look to the other provinces for assistance as they seek to develop sufficient financial and leadership resources. In recent years Native American Moravians in California have come together with indigenous Moravians in Alaska and Labrador for "first nations' outreach."

EASTERN WEST INDIES

The Eastern West Indies Province includes the Virgin Islands of the United States, St. Kitts, Antigua, Barbados, and Trinidad-Tobago, with headquarters in Antigua. Approximately 19,000 members are contained in the 50 congregations. St Thomas marked the beginning of Moravian missions worldwide in 1732. This inaugurated a new dimension for all Protestantism, as other European denominations followed.

The story of the early struggles between missionaries and West Indian planters is well told in a modern film, *The First Fruits*. Books and shorter publications rehearse the same story and its gradual fruit — the souls of black slaves not given their civil freedom for another century.

British and German missionaries were the first to serve in the West Indies. In the 1900s, especially after World War II, the American provinces were called upon to furnish pastors, teachers, and temporary specialists such as Christian education teachers, but today all of the leadership is West Indian.

The Eastern West Indies Province is one that has long taken ecumenical ministry seriously. One current example is a united Moravian – Presbyterian – Methodist congregation in that province.

The migration to Great Britain, the United States, and Canada of many West Indians has helped to forge ties between islands and mainland. This exchange of faith and fellowship is very significant in the life of the church in the 21st century.

MORAVIANS TODAY

EASTER; GOD'S ACRE

Easter time is special to all Christians; and early morning services are held in virtually every American community. There are several unusual elements in the Moravian way, however. One is the Easter Morning Liturgy, read and affirmed as a confession of faith. This strikes people as especially appropriate since the resurrection was the climax of Christ's coming. Another characteristic that is most likely uniquely Moravian is to start the service indoors before dawn and conclude in a graveyard as the sun rises. This began in 1732 in Germany when a group of young men spontaneously agreed to make their way to God's Acre (as Moravians called the cemetery) "toward the dawn of the first day of the week (Matthew 28:1 RSV)." Only the older Moravian churches, with an exception or two, have their own graveyards, but the tradition is continued, even if the service must be held indoors.

In Winston-Salem, North Carolina, tens of thousands of worshipers gather in the Salem Square as the night of Great Sabbath ends. A quiet reverence prevails, broken only by the sound of Moravian musicians playing wind instruments in groups here and there across the city. Easter chorales remind listeners to gather in front of the church for the age-old proclamation "The Lord is risen," to which all will respond, "The Lord is risen indeed."

Like other Moravians, West Indians love to sing. In some congregations they chant the "Te Deum Laudamus" with heartiness and musical finesse. They tend to be more liturgical in their preferences than most African-American Moravians.

This migration has truly enriched the Northern and Southern Provinces, perhaps most notably at Synods and conferences. At least 15 pastors from the West Indies and Central America (including three bishops) bring strong gifts of leadership to these provinces.

As the service continues and the crowd moves to God's Acre, the bands play antiphonally from various corners and finally merge, 400-members strong. The effect of so many instruments heralding the life everlasting is powerful.

People in orderly columns line the walkways between the rows and rows of graves, all with simple, uniform, flat white stones. The scene is evidence of the democracy of death. Loved ones, survivors, have placed flowers on each grave, tokens of faith in the life to come.

The use of brass and reed instruments at Easter is consistent with the Moravian view of death. A person dying in the faith has not reached the end, but only the portal to an eternity in God's presence. So this is appropriately heralded with trumpets and joy. The stirring words, "The day of resurrection, Earth tell it out abroad," are supported with triumphant music.

**God's Acre,
Winston-Salem, NC**

43

THE CARIBBEAN RING

If one starts in Puerto Rico and draws a clockwise semi-circle to Venezuela, a ring of places where Moravians are at work is traceable. First there are the Virgin Islands and the formerly British Islands just mentioned. Then, to the east of Venezuela is Guyana and next to that, Suriname. Both are countries with Moravian churches, along with Jamaica (south of Cuba), Nicaragua, Honduras, and Costa Rica in Central America. In the Dominican Republic (west of Puerto Rico) the Moravian Church joined hands with the United Methodists and Presbyterians to help form a federation of Protestant churches.

The missionary outreach of the eighteenth and nineteenth centuries was primarily to the less educated and less developed nations, commonly called the Third World. Today the Caribbean ring of Moravian provinces beyond the Eastern West Indies embraces more than 100,000 members in five provinces. The largest is Nicaragua. Here well-known political conditions in the 1980s made the work of the church very difficult.

Political power resides on the west coast among people of Spanish (mestizo) and Creole descent. Moravians minister primarily to the Miskitu and Mayangna indigenous people on the east coast. There is only one congregation on the west coast, in Managua; it has weathered all kinds of political upheavals and earthquakes. Most of the members have come to Managua from the east coast.

UNCERTAINTY IN NICARAGUA

The Moravian Church of Nicaragua had just become self-sustaining and staffed by indigenous leadership when the revolution came in 1979. Sadly, as the new Sandinista government expanded its activities in the Atlantic Coast area, many Indian people found reason for increasing concern about protection of traditional land and cultural rights on the east coast. As conflict escalated and as the Nicaraguan government carried out a forced evacuation of the villages along the Coco River, between Nicaragua and Honduras, thousands of Indian people, most of them Moravians, were dislocated. An estimated 5,000 fled to Costa Rica, and another 25,000 went across the Rio Coco into Honduras.

The years since then have seen rising and falling political stability. The vital Nicaraguan Province continues to deal with Christian witness in a changing environment. Current activity includes the building of churches in villages where Moravians have resettled and reestablishing a theological study center at Puerto Cabezas (Bilwi) and a hospital at Bilwaskarma.

RELIEF PROJECTS

When the level of conflict subsided, some Nicaragua Moravians elected to stay in Honduras, but the need for supplies of clothing, food, medicine, and cash continued for years. In addition, devastating hurricanes in 1988, 1999, and 2007 provided opportunities for partnership in the face of deep human need.

The Moravian witness abroad has consistently begun with evangelism, but it always broadens according to need. A social action group began in Nicaragua in the 1970s and continues as ADSIM (The Agency for Social Development of the Moravian Church in Nicaragua). Ministry to the whole person is the Christian aim.

Every decade brings new application of this principle, as well as ever-stronger links among provinces. This is illustrated by the development of new congregations in Miami, Florida, consisting of many immigrant Nicaraguans. Also in the early 1990s a native of Nicaragua served as the treasurer of the Board of World Mission in Bethlehem, Pennsylvania.

HONDURAS AND COSTA RICA

North of Nicaragua is the Honduran Province, augmented in the 1980s by 7,000-8,000 of the refugees from the Rio Coco area of Nicaragua. During the 1990s a strong charismatic movement developed within the province, bringing with it both benefits and challenges.

A clinic, hospital, and two full-time resident physicians (one of whom is a native Honduran) are located in Ahuas, and a second clinic in Cauquira serves the people of that area. In recent years Americans have assisted in the specialized areas of theology, economic development, and Christian education.

Another aspect of growth in the Honduran church is the establishment of new churches outside La Mosquitia, its traditional area of work. Many of the new members are Hispanic, not Miskitu, and a new ministry has begun among the Garifuna people (Black Caribs) in northeast Honduras and the port of La Ceiba. Mission outreach from Honduras is also taking place in the neighboring country of Belize.

Finally, Costa Rica, south of Nicaragua, has more than half a dozen congregations and was approved in 1988 as a new Moravian province. Current members are primarily Nicaraguan immigrants and refugees, but new outreach is among the Costa Rican population.

JAMAICA, CAYMAN ISLANDS, AND CUBA

To most Americans, Jamaica means basking in the winter sunshine of Montego Bay and listening to rhythmic reggae music. Or maybe they have heard of Kingston, on the other side of the island, where more of the national action is — the seat of government, the University of the West Indies, and (as it turns out) the headquarters of the Moravian Church.

Jamaica is the third largest island of the Caribbean and a land of extraordinary beauty. Moravians have been at work there since 1754, about 100 years after it was conquered by the British. The original inhabitants were Arawak Indians, but two British planters asked Moravian missionaries to come to evangelize and instruct their slaves from Africa.

Education thus became a prime objective of the church. Its extension is the present Bethlehem Teachers' College, in the rural highlands, and the support (jointly with the Eastern West Indies Province) of a chair in the United Theological College at the University. The Bethlehem College spreads its influence out into government schools across the island, while most Caribbean Moravian ministers are trained at the University.

In the comfortable climate of the Jamaica highlands, churches with a variety of biblical and other names minister faithfully: Mandeville, Nazareth, Carmel, and Malvern. Unitas is an agency of the church engaged in a variety of social service projects. It sponsors medical and dental clinics, and agricultural services. Now a new challenge faces the province: a "mission" to the nearby Grand Cayman islands, where Nicaraguans and Jamaicans have been migrating. In turn, Moravians in the Caymans assist in nurturing a small but growing group in Cuba.

The ecumenical Caribbean Council of Churches looks for ways (with some North American support) to raise the economic life of both Jamaica and other islands. Poverty in the Third World is ever present, next to the luxury of the tourist trade and the hazardous bauxite industry.

SURINAME AND GUYANA

Suriname, on the north shore of South America, is a small nation; but its approximately 45,000 Moravians exert a prominent influence. They are found among all the racial strains: Maroons (or Bush Negroes), Arawak Indians, Javanese, Chinese, East Indians, and the mixed Dutch-Africans. Along with many churches, children's homes and 70 schools (with 20,000 pupils) have been established. Moravians in a joint venture with Lutherans and Dutch Reformed also operate a hospital in Paramaribo.

Paramaribo, the capital city, has a Moravian church with the largest membership in the world. In addition it has the *Stadzending* and the unique Kersten and Company store. The former is "mission to the city," and houses a coffee shop, bookstore, radio studios, and conference rooms, with ample meeting space. Kersten is an overgrown country store, now like a shopping mall. It is part of a large holding company and includes a retail center where you can buy anything from a needle to a tractor.

Moravian numbers in Guyana are only around 1,000, but one new congregation was started recently, and young people are deciding for the Christian ministry. In Queenstown the church serves hot lunches to schoolchildren; and in South Ruimveldt an agri-project utilizes three lots next to the church. The province also witnesses to its faith through a radio broadcast.

Guyana's greatest problems are economic, so that Christian ministry cannot be one-sided. The political situation has become stabilized after considerable upheaval that followed the country's becoming independent under the British Commonwealth. Over the 250 years of Moravian outreach into many lands, problems and change have come to be the norm. Yet somehow survival has been a blessing to the faithful!

THE MORAVIAN CHURCH FOUNDATION

Some years ago the Moravian Church Foundation was established as an agency of the Moravian Unity to supervise Kersten and several other Unity business enterprises. Funds from these businesses are used to support theological training throughout the Unity as well as many special projects. A significant portion of the proceeds assists the Suriname province, land of the Foundation's origin, in its many ministries.

OVERVIEW

This would seem to be a good place to enumerate five points emphasized by the Rev. Theodore Wilde, former executive director of the Board of World Mission of the Moravian Church in America. He makes these points as an overview of Moravianism across the globe today and also as a reflection on mission methodology as contrasted to over 250 years ago.

1. While the Moravian Church is a Unity, customs and practices of the numerous provinces vary immensely. For example, in Tanzania the dead are always buried with the head to the west, to rise and face eastward toward the returning Christ. Also in Tanzania, Moravians dance in celebration and praise to God when a bishop is consecrated. (This would add variety to an American consecration service!)

2. Moravian unity is secured relationally, not administratively. The church enjoys more uniformity than some communions just because it does not try to squeeze everyone into the same mold.

3. Moravian church government reflects a policy of order and freedom. It is democratic in form, with key synodal elections conducted without nomination and without advance politicking.

4. In the newly independent provinces there is a strong interest in local forms as expressions of the Christian faith. There is more recognition of native spiritual gifts than there was two centuries ago. The piety then expressed tended to be more uniformly European or North American.

RETURNING TO EUROPE

It has been noted that a special ingredient of Moravian fellowship is learning to know other Moravians by touring. European centers of the church are at the top of the list, beginning with Herrnhut.

In eastern Germany, Herrnhut today is more than just a Moravian town. More non-Moravians live there than Moravians, but 600 or so members of the church keep their traditions and pursue a quiet, spiritually-oriented life. They still think of themselves as a "church within a church," as Zinzendorf developed it. This was his principle of trying to bring spiritual renewal within the state church, rather than leaving it entirely and starting a new denomination.

The church edifice and several other Herrnhut buildings were burned by Russian soldiers in the last days of World War II, but were gradually restored. Some Moravian buildings now house a school for mentally handicapped children and adults. A number of the handicapped young people have asked the church for Christian baptism — a reason for special joy in an increasingly secular and thus sometimes apparently hostile land.

A modified version of the "choir system" prevails in the town, by which the single sisters, married people, and widows meet for spiritual nurture and to celebrate their choir days annually. In the case of the single women, a separate building with individual apartments is available; but communal living is a thing of the past.

TEXTS DRAWN

The archives detailing the renewal of the denomination is in the Moravian part of town. Nearby, the *Daily Texts* (Losungen) for each year are carefully drawn in solemn ceremony.

The church in the eastern part of Germany is small — only ten congregations with 2,600 total members, but the Moravian influence is much broader than appearances would indicate. A Diaspora work continues, as

The *Daily Texts* are drawn from this silver bowl in Germany.

traveling evangelists from both eastern and western Germany circulate among the state churches, bearing mission news and gathering support for enterprises of the Unity in Albania, Latvia, Africa, North India, and Palestine.

Zinzendorf's grave in Herrnhut

As one walks a short mile out of Herrnhut, the cemetery (God's Acre) stands out, with its arbored pathways, its flat gravestones, and the elevated stones marking the graves of the Zinzendorf family. Then one passes the manor house where the count lived, and finally Berthelsdorf and the Lutheran parish church. With its quaint belfry and chaste white interior, the sanctuary seems still to want to rehearse the experience of August 13, 1727, when the brothers and sisters felt a unique outpouring of the Holy Spirit. That is when the ancient Moravian Church was reborn.

The Zinzendorf manor house

A RESORT TURNED CLINIC

A major bequest brought the church in western Germany a health resort and hotel at Bad Boll, in the Stuttgart area. The "Kurhaus" and spa had been used at one time by the king of Wuerttemburg. In order to meet the needs of a different population, the church turned the spa into a rehabilitation clinic. Although the church no longer operates the clinic, it is only a short distance from the headquarters of the European Continental Province, all of which comprises a single picturesque community. The Bad Boll congregation still worships at the Kurhaus. An interdenominational conference center in another part of Bad Boll, made famous by the ministry of the Blumhardt family, gives the community a distinctly ecumenical flavor as well.

The Bad Boll headquarters coordinates Moravian work in Holland, Denmark, Sweden, Switzerland, and all of the German congregations, east and west. At Koenigsfeld, in the Black Forest, the church operates two fine boarding schools and ministers to the community with a strong congregation.

In Koenigsfeld one can also visit a house where the famous Albert Schweitzer lived for a time. Neuwied on the Rhine below Heidelberg is likewise a Moravian center with an active youth program and a comfortable home for the elderly.

The Swiss headquarters for a small Moravian work is in Basle. Christiansfeld in Denmark bears more marks of a settlement congregation like Herrnhut. It is the headquarters for the modest ministry of the church in Denmark. For their size, Danish Moravians have exerted a tremendous influence in missionary work, especially in Tanzania.

IN THE NETHERLANDS

Zeist is southwest of Utrecht and not too far from Naarden, where by an accident of history the remains of the great educator and Moravian bishop John Amos Comenius are interred. The Moravian section of Zeist was laid out in the 1700s in the grand style of Zinzendorf. The "palace," now used as the center for Holland's national park and museum service, commands the distant south end of the 15- or 20-acre park. A tree-lined, neatly trimmed driveway leads to it, with church buildings still in use on either side.

To the right is a spacious quadrangle of brick buildings, including the church sanctuary. Apartments for families as well as single persons are a major portion of the adjacent buildings and across the huge terrace on the left. Companion brick buildings and apartments grace the well-manicured lawns there also. Among the residents have been retired missionaries and ministers, some of whom served in Suriname.

One other building, a residence for Surinamese students studying in Holland, stands at the right side of the driveway leading to the main complex. Finally, a large factory employing scores of workers and supporting Moravian enterprises has been located on the back area of the tract.

As mentioned elsewhere, the membership of the Moravian Church in the Netherlands has been augmented considerably by Surinamese immigrants. Services are held in Amsterdam, Rotterdam, and Utrecht for these seemingly permanent residents. This is but one of many places where the "sending congregations" of the 1700s have become "receiving congregations" with the result of increased vitality and strength.

HOMELAND OF THE UNITY

Political conditions never seem to favor the faithful in the Moravian homeland, the Czech Republic. There was national independence for 20 years after World War I. Then Hitler moved into the Sudetenland. From 1945-1948 the Benes regime began setting up a democracy, only to suffer a Russian takeover. This was three centuries after Bishop Comenius and his band of companions fled to Poland. Religious toleration is always at the mercy of politics and Czech politics have been cruel.

It was a friendly Austrian government that allowed the Moravian Church to start anew at Potstejn (Pottenstein), 120 miles southeast of Prague, in 1870. A dozen other congregations were subsequently organized in rural Bohemia, one in Moravia, and eventually a "chapel and headquarters" in Prague. The members are a cheerful band of humble and devoted Christians resolved to maintain a Czech province of the church, regardless of the struggle.

Visitors from overseas are welcomed enthusiastically to the homeland. When the 1967 Unity Synod was held at Potstejn, delegates were entertained with a hospitality that seemed far beyond what the humble lifestyle of the members might allow. It was, for the Czechs, a time of refreshment just before the Dubcek ouster. The warmth of Christian fellowship, mutually exchanged, surmounted all barriers of language, culture, or politics.

A visitor from North America may see the tiny restored chapel at Kunwald, where the Unitas Fratrum began in 1457. Zelezny Brod, the town famous for its blown glass, has one of the province's finest sanctuaries. It houses a pipe organ dedicated in a recital by Albert Schweitzer, and is now a civic hall for concerts and other events.

A warm welcome will be given to fellow Christians at the church in Mlada Boleslav, the town where the Skoda car is made; at ancient Potstejn; or high in the mountains at Tanvald. Also, no one who has seen them will ever forget the Chalice Rocks where the faithful hid during days of persecution, singing to the God who is the Rock of Ages.

Chalice Rocks

Being a Christian in the Czech Republic is never easy. After the "Velvet Revolution" in 1989 the Czech church (the Jednota Bratrská) experienced a noticeable revival in some of its congregations due to the charismatic movement. The 1992 international conference of Moravian bishops, meeting in Nova Paka, was sufficiently impressed that it gave the revival its blessing. Czech Moravians have been active in mission outreach and service among gypsies, orphans, urban dwellers, and many others.

IN BRITAIN

Methodists and many other Protestants have heard of Aldersgate and know about John Wesley's pivotal experience of having his "heart strangely warmed." This was in London, and many of the group around Wesley were Moravians. The latter had been in England for nearly ten years, partly because of ties between Zinzendorf and royal advisers to George I.

Schools in Fulneck, Yorkshire, and Ockbrook, Derbyshire, represent some of the chief influence of the Moravian Church in England today. Restoration is underway also at Fairfield, near Manchester, where schools were established as early as 1783. Had the Moravians been as skillful and zealous organizers as Wesley, there would probably be far more than the approximately 1,700 adherents now numbered by the Moravian Church in England and Northern Ireland. But the early emphasis was always on evangelism within the state church. Moravians had no heart for being separatists or sectarians.

Despite their small numbers, British Moravians are still mission minded. Over the years they have contributed heavily to the Unity's work in Labrador, the Eastern West Indies, Jamaica, and western Tanzania. They support generously the church and schools in North India and Nepal, as well as the joint undertaking at Star Mountain in Palestine. Another development in Britain is the presence now of five congregations composed largely of Moravians from the West Indies.

SOUTH AFRICA AND ITS BURDEN

Moravians have been in South Africa since 1737 and were among the many people of goodwill whose gratitude overflowed when this great nation finally abolished apartheid and gave voting rights to all in 1994. Now the African church members can see tangible fruit from their steady influence to bring about equality, freedom, and mutual respect.

Because of the pattern of historic mission work, Moravians in South Africa are mostly people of color. People are of mixed ethnic background: descendants of white settlers, Khoikhoi and San Bushmen, and East Indian and African slaves. They speak Afrikaans (a language related to Dutch) and also English.

There are Moravians in Cape Town, but the older congregations in the Western Cape area are in the agricultural hinterland. The oldest mission station in Southern Africa is Genadendal, "valley of grace." This settlement is reminiscent of Herrnhut, Salem, and other early Moravian communities. Today it is an active congregation, but also an interesting museum and heritage center. In 1995, President Nelson Mandela announced that his official residence in Cape Town was renamed Genadendal in order to symbolize that the State President serves under God's grace, just as Moravians had for centuries.

Church schools are still important in South Africa. A treatment center for mentally and physically handicapped children and young people is known as the Moravian Elim Home. Outside aid from state and other agencies like Rotary International provides support for Elim and also the many daycare centers for working mothers. These are known as "creches." Obviously with economic pressures what they are on ministries in South Africa, daycare is a vital service.

The total strength of the South African church is about 100,000, and it stands in solidarity with both the South Africa Council of Churches and the Federation of Evangelical Lutheran Churches in South Africa. The latter is a unique relationship and reflects the origin of Moravian missions in the German state church. About 40 part-time and full-time students are enrolled at the Moravian Theological Center at Heideveld, Cape Town, which also houses the Moravian Archives.

Clearly the burdens of these fellow Christians are the legacies of nearly 50 years of apartheid. The "new" South Africa is plagued by high unemployment, widespread illiteracy, and the very uneven distribution of wealth. There are old political wounds to be healed. These conditions hamper church development. While apartheid has been legally abolished, attitudes shaped by it remain in the hearts of many people. A tremendous amount of goodwill and commitment to a free and just future displayed by peoples of all racial backgrounds is the attitude of present day South Africa.

TANZANIA, THE BROADEST PILLAR

The largest wild animal preserve in the world is in the fascinating East African country known as Tanzania. It is a country of unique beauty and is governed by a particular brand of socialism. It seems to walk a circumspect path between East and West. The name Tanzania comes from a blending of the old Tanganyika and Zanzibar.

Tanzanian children carry goods from a food bank

To Moravians the large animal preserve is less important than the fact that here is the fastest growing branch of the Unitas Fratrum. It is also the largest in membership. The total membership is over 400,000 — more than half of the constituency of the worldwide Moravian Church. This seems to be the place to say that 90% of Moravians the world over are people of color, the happy result of missionary efforts begun in 1732.

Tanzania, with its four component provinces, is symbolic, in that over the years Moravians from Canada, the United States, Great Britain, and Europe have shared in providing financial and personnel support. Numerous gifted Tanzanian pastors have taken graduate or undergraduate studies at Moravian Theological Seminary in Bethlehem, Pennsylvania, and have gone on to assume important leadership roles, not only in their respective provinces, but also in the Unity as a whole. From 2001 to 2004 the President of the worldwide Unity Board was from Tanzania.

RAPID GROWTH

The rapid growth of the Moravian Church and other Christian bodies in Tanzania seems to contradict the impression that the Muslim religion is sweeping through Africa. With the breakdown of trust in animism, the vacuum is filled by other religions. So far Muslims and Christians live in a degree of mutual respect.

For the Moravians the population feels a particular trust because of continuing service in medicine and education. As long as the government provides a stable environment, growth of the church should continue. Swahili is the national language, but many study English as well.

Work among lepers in Tanzania began in 1904 and is still unfinished today, although the number of cases is tapering off. The Kidugallo leper settlement is affiliated with the Moravian hospital in Sikonge and has been serving since 1923. Malaria continues to take an enormous toll in Africa, and of course the AIDS epidemic brings tragedy into every community. The Tanzanian church has mounted a comprehensive AIDS education program and provides care for AIDS patients. Perhaps the greatest need is to care for the tens of thousands of AIDS orphans, a task undertaken in partnership with European and North American Moravians.

Moravian care is always for the whole person. Church, school, and clinic or hospital go together. An example of this is Mbeya in southwest Tanzania, east of the southern tip of Lake Tanganyika. There, near the headquarters of the Southwestern Province is the Teofilo Kisanji University and Theological College, as well as an elementary school and a medical center.

To facilitate the rapid expansion of the Tanzanian church, four separately governed provinces have been formed under a comprehensive Moravian Church in Tanzania: the Western, Southern, Southwestern, and Rukwa. In addition, the church is extending its mission outreach to the southwest (Zambia), to the south (Malawi), to northeast Tanzania and Zanzibar, and to both Rwanda and Kenya. There are over 13,000 Moravians in the emerging work in the Democratic Republic of Congo. A thriving Internet café helps finance the church's ministry there.

The future, therefore, is bright in East Africa. Fortunately indigenous leadership seems to be generated in proportion to the opportunities. How great are the mysteries of the God who made the first missionaries to what was then German East Africa wait six years for their first convert, 1891-1897!

5

FELLOWSHIP AND PRACTICES

Moravian customs give members of the church a sense of identity. They are an emotional matter. As someone once remarked, "Never take these away from me." At their best, customs are part of the fabric of people's spiritual living. When practiced again and again, they foster a special kind of fellowship among those who share them.

One woman underscores Moravian fellowship as a shared experience. "Wherever I go," she would say, "I feel I have much to share, to give, and to receive — with any other Moravian." This is an intangible — hard to describe, but deeply felt.

The value of fellowship is clear on the local scene. It is also evident when an anniversary occasion is celebrated, or during a mission festival, a groundbreaking, or a church dedication. Groups of Moravians travel to other churches to share in the celebration. (When a new church was dedicated in Arizona, a whole caravan, complete with trombone choir, traveled 350 miles from California to join in the important event.)

In the outlined boxes interspersed throughout this book we have described quite a few customs and practices. It is appropriate to ask now whether members of the faith are open to new ideas or keep the church's life and practice fixed in stone.

NEW IDEAS

Actually this is a mixed pattern. Some changes have come with relative ease. For instance, there are now quite a number of women clergy in the church, a growing percentage in both parish work and specialized ministries. Predominantly white congregations have begun to call black clergy as pastors.

Again, when the charismatic movement swept through the Christian churches of America, Moravians accepted certain elements (not usually speaking in tongues) and felt a general quickening from it. Today one sees continuing influence in some congregations. Examples include prominence of intercessory prayer both in Sunday worship and in home groups, and the use of praise music, occasionally sung by worshipers with uplifted hands. Another example of flexibility is the introduction of new liturgies into the worship of the church.

COVENANT

A unique document, *The Moravian Covenant for Christian Living,* deserves full examination by serious students of the Moravian faith. It is a 34-point statement of desirable ethical and religious practice with roots back to the time of Zinzendorf and the so-called settlement congregations, in which only Moravians lived.

Some elements of the code have been likened to the *Ratio Disciplinae* framed by Bishop Comenius in the 1600s. The current document is a revision made in the 1960s and amended occasionally since then. It has been officially adopted by both North American provinces.

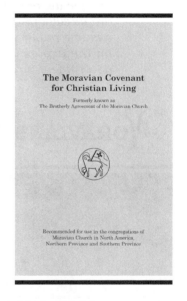

The Moravian Covenant
for Christian Living

Formerly known as
The Brotherly Agreement of the Moravian Church

Recommended for use in the congregations of
Moravian Church in North America,
Northern Province and Southern Province

In a period when divorce rates are high and stable home life seems threatened by an endless stream of obstacles, what guidance is given to Moravians?

> *We regard Christian marriage as an indissoluble union, which requires the lifelong loyalty of the man and woman toward each other... If at any time the stability of their marriage is threatened, they are to seek the counsel of their pastor or other spiritual leaders in the Church as soon as possible and before any other action is taken.*

TEMPERANCE; CIVIL DISOBEDIENCE

Where does the church stand on the use of alcohol? Has it spoken to the issues of drug abuse or smoking? Paragraph 30 of the *Covenant* reads in part:

> *We are aware of the problems that can be caused by the intemperate use of such things as alcoholic beverages, food, tobacco, drugs. We regard intemperance in any area of living as being inconsistent with the Christian life.*

Moravians consider it a "special privilege to live in a democratic society," so members are expected

> *to fulfill the responsibilities of our citizenship, among which are intelligent and well-informed voting, a willingness to assume public office, guiding the decisions of government by the expression of our opinions, and supporting good government by our personal efforts.*

ℳ︎ORAVIANS TODAY

Daily Text cards, kept in Germany

DAILY DEVOTIONS

In many Moravian homes there is a little book on the breakfast table, next to the orange juice, toast, and coffee. It is the *Daily Texts*. Either aloud or silently the selection for the day is read from a single page: an Old Testament verse with a hymn stanza, fitting the verse; a New Testament verse on a related theme, with its matching hymn selection; and a brief prayer for the day.

Some Moravian customs were born centuries ago. This one began on May 3, 1728, and has endured. On that evening their patron, Count Zinzendorf, gave the congregation at Herrnhut, Germany, a watchword for the next day. Messengers regularly thereafter relayed a text for each new day to the 32 houses of the settlement. By 1731 there was a printed edition, *Losungen*, issued to help people grow in their devotional lives.

Civil disobedience as such is not mentioned in the code, but there is recognition that in addition to necessary loyalty to the state, a Christian has a higher loyalty to God and conscience.

In their early years on this continent Moravians were pacifists. This principle gave way by the time of the Civil War to the privilege of each member's following his or her own conscience as to military service. Sadly, church members were drawn into the conflict on both sides. The denomination has always stood by all members who for reasons of conscience feel war is wrong and object to military service.

Today the little book is printed in 51 languages and dialects on five continents. Over a million copies are printed in German alone, even though there are only 20,000 members of the Moravian Church in all of Europe. Clearly this little book has been used mightily to help people all over the world to face a new day.

Numerous striking coincidences are recorded about how the *Daily Texts* sounded just the right note when the day for their use arrived. For instance, on July 4, 1776, the watchword was Isaiah 55:5 — "Behold, you shall call nations that you knew not, and nations that knew you not shall run to you." And this text had been selected by lot in Germany a year before that!

Many well-known people have used and cherished the little devotional book. German Dietrich Bonhoeffer, down to the day when Hitler marched him from his prison cell to his execution, read the *Losungen* and commented on them in his diary. The mad dictator knew Bonhoeffer was among those plotting to overthrow him, but "the Word of God is not bound." Bonhoeffer lives on in glory! Hitler died in infamy.

CHURCH DISCIPLINE

This is a delicate subject among all Christians. To what degree is any religious body warranted in limiting people's freedom, especially one that in its motto says, "In non-essentials, liberty"?

When a Brotherly Agreement (the forerunner of today's *Moravian Covenant for Christian Living*) was written over 200 years ago, many Moravians lived in a closed community. Considerable conformity in behavior was expected, and elder-counselors were in close touch with "higher ups" in the denomination. Any such close surveillance of behavior would be unthinkable to North Americans today, but the final paragraph of the *Covenant* reads:

> *We make it a duty of the Board of Elders, which is charged with the spiritual welfare of the Congregation, to see that this 'Moravian Covenant' be adhered to and faithfully observed; and we will cooperate with the Board of Elders in its efforts to maintain the discipline of the congregation.*

> *As a redemptive community we will be much more concerned with aiding than censuring those who alter, being conscious of our own need for correction and forgiveness.*

It should be clear from the last sentence that Moravians don't approach anything like the practice of "shunning." Seldom is a church member today denied the privilege of Holy Communion; and being dismissed from church membership for moral reasons is rare.

PRIOR ASSUMPTIONS

The earlier paragraphs of the *Covenant* are more theological, dealing with "The Ground of Our Witness," and specifically "The Witness of the Christian Life." Here one finds a brief statement on baptism and emphasis on the fact that the earliest of Christian confessions contained four words only: "Jesus Christ is Lord." This is consistent with what was stated in chapter 3, What Moravians Believe. Coequal with the heavenly Father, Jesus is to be obeyed as the supportive Ruler and Lord of believers' lives.

Here is a tall order, but the *Covenant* also recognizes that human beings can live the Christian life only with God's help. Hence the encouragement to practice daily devotions. Furthermore, stewardship is a serious matter, as to time, talents, and financial resources.

When it comes to the Moravian worldwide Unity, congregations and individuals are to see themselves as part of the whole. Moreover, good stewardship leads to the support of worthy causes outside the church as well as inside.

SETTLE OUTSIDE THE COURT

Church members are to "cherish Christian love as of prime importance" and are to be known for their mutual love in Christ. Divisive issues are to be expected; but they should be settled in love among the church family. "We will endeavor to settle our differences with others in a Christian manner, amicably, and with mediation, and if at all possible avoid resort to a court of law."

Other paragraphs of the Covenant deal with:

* Faithful attendance at Sunday worship.

* Keeping Sunday as free from labor as possible.

* The special importance of Holy Communion.

* Fellowship with other Christians.

* Treatment of all persons without hatred, slander, or injury.

* Recognition that "discrimination based on color, race, creed, or land of origin" is contrary to God's will.

The code is obviously not all-inclusive, but it defines the nature of attainable Christian living. Contemporary church emphasis on evangelism makes up for what might seem to be missing in that area. However, the Moravian spirit is still to avoid proselytizing. The gospel is to be proclaimed with prayer and enthusiasm but never with the intention of overwhelming a possible convert.

6

ℐOVERNMENT OF THE MORAVIAN CHURCH

When church members think of what the church is, they tend to center on the local church. While this is certainly true for Moravians as well, they really have something unusual in their worldwide Unity. This is a closely-knit federation of more than 20 provinces on four continents. Every seven years a Unity synod is convened with three delegates from each of the established provinces and one delegate each from the so-called affiliated provinces: those not yet completely self-supporting.

Worship, study, fellowship, and committee work comprise the agenda along with legislative sessions. Individual provinces agree to be bound by the synodal decisions, and sessions last about two weeks. A typical assortment of issues discussed would be:

- Recognition of new provinces, some in process of development, and some moving from affiliated to fully indigenous status. For instance, the congregations and schools in South Asia (North India and Nepal) are being evaluated to see whether they should become an affiliated province.

- Concern for justice, peace, the integrity of creation — all in the context of differing political and economic systems.

- Theological education and how the church can better respond to theological and political developments in its provinces.

- So-called "Unity Undertakings," where joint support is given to projects outside the provinces, through offerings of the congregations. Or investigation may be initiated prior to the establishment of efforts at new witness. In this century naturally this calls for the raising of new millions of dollars.

- Matters related to confirmation, Holy Communion, and the orders of the ministry. For example, the 1988 Unity Synod voted to allow children to be admitted to Holy Communion prior to confirmation in provinces wishing to follow this practice.

Between synods a Unity Board functions as the executive body, mostly by correspondence. This includes a representative from the provincial board of each province; and the presidency rotates. From time to time Unity conferences may be called; and the Unity Board meets at least twice between synods depending on available finances.

No matter what legislation comes out of Unity synods, strong international fellowship results, and better understanding of mutual problems. The sessions also lead to new, assisting relationships such as the ones the American provinces have had to Alaska, Labrador, Guyana, Nicaragua, Honduras, the Eastern West Indies, and Western Tanzania.

CLOSER TO HOME

The Northern and Southern Provinces are self-governing under the Unity Synod. They function in essentially identical fashion and meet in legislative sessions (synods) every four years. Also, the North has three districts, each of which has a synod and district conference every four years. The district synods are usually convened halfway through the provincial synod cycle. They elect their executive boards (lay and clergy), along with other district officials. District conferences (non-legislative) occur at the call of the district executive boards.

And what is the work of a provincial synod? It elects its executive board (the Provincial Elders' Conference, lay and clergy members) and bishops. It gives oversight and direction to all provincial agencies and institutions and elects their boards, examining also the financial status of each. It gives direction for church publication needs, plans for the church's witness in the years ahead, and hears any complaints or grievances of congregations or individual members.

General supervision is given to the congregations by the synods, and in the North to the districts also. Reports by the bundle, of course, are brought to the synods for action; and bundles more are taken back to the congregations and agencies for implementation.

Most synods fashion programs for the intersynodal years, some of them financial, others for church growth, youth work, camping, or social action. Considerable confidence in the Lord's leading is attached to the synod election of provincial elders and bishops, without nomination or campaign speeches.

BOARDS AND COMMISSIONS

A chart of provincial boards and service agencies in the Northern Province would look much the same in the South. Both provinces take Christian education in the local church very seriously. Boards and commissions work with the Sunday schools and Vacation Bible schools all year long. Each province also operates one or more camps and one or more retirement communities. A monthly magazine, *The Moravian*, serves both provinces and is delivered to every Moravian home as a privilege of membership.

Moravian schools and colleges are virtually autonomous, although church-related. They also receive financial support from the districts and provinces — major support for Moravian Theological Seminary, minor support for the other institutions.

ORDERS OF THE MINISTRY

Moravians have preserved the historic three orders of church: deacon, presbyter (priest), and bishop. These do not form a hierarchy; and the bishops by virtue of their offices have no dioceses or administrative authority. That is vested in the provincial elders' conferences and the district boards.

Deacons are ordained by bishops, almost always after obtaining a degree in theology and after qualifying before a committee of review. They must have a call to pastoral or other Christian service before ordination takes place. They have full privileges to preach, administer the sacraments, and do the pastoral and administrative work described in their calls. The latter are issued by the Provincial Elders' Conference "in the name of Jesus Christ, the Head of the Church."

After a probationary period of three to five years, deacons are consecrated presbyters of the church by a bishop. This demonstrates the approval of the local congregation or agency served, that of the district board (where applicable), and that of the church at large. For a presbyter, no additional functions beyond that of a deacon are usually involved.

Bishops in the Moravian Church are a symbol of the continuity of the Unitas Fratrum. Their line has been unbroken from 1467. Elected for life, they perform all ordinations and ministerial consecrations, and are primarily spiritual leaders of the church. They are counselors and pastors of pastors. They offer intercession for the entire Unity and are bishops wherever they travel or reside. The American Northern Province in 1998 moved forward in a new direction by electing the first female bishop of the Unity, the Rt. Rev. Kay Ward. Since that time, several other female bishops have been elected in various provinces.

GETTING A NEW MINISTER

If you are a Methodist or Episcopalian, you are accustomed to having your minister appointed (on recommendation, of course). If you happen to be a Baptist or Disciple of Christ, your local congregation or board engages the minister. Other denominations use variations of these systems. Since Moravian Church government is conferential, the procedure runs like this:

1. The Provincial Elders' Conference or District Board is charged with taking the initiatives when a pastoral vacancy occurs. It arranges a meeting with the elders and trustees (the governing boards) of the vacant congregation to discuss the church's needs; and this local board (not the membership at large) represents the congregation's voice. No candidating is done by prospective pastors and no vote of the congregation at large is ever taken.

2. Candidates for the pastoral offices are nominated by the provincial or district board; and local board members are free to propose additional brothers or sisters.

3. Full and open discussion of all prospects is engaged. Then a vote for first choice is cast. Naturally the objective is to get "just the right man or woman," matching the congregation's needs with the pastor's skills.

4. The process usually takes two months or more; and after the call is issued, the final decision rests with the person called. Often a pastor holding a call meets with the joint board involved; but pastors are seldom pressured to accept, and neither the local or denominational board can be forced by the other to call any one candidate. The whole system rests on mutual confidence.

Terms of the call are carefully defined, again by mutual agreement. If the first call is declined, the process is repeated until a call is accepted. Separation from the pastor's previous position is accomplished within a month or so, and then installation occurs.

A pastor may live in the congregation-owned parsonage or be provided with a housing allowance for selection of his or her own quarters. All pastors are covered with a health policy and start qualifying for pensions after a designated period of service.

LOCAL CONGREGATIONAL STRUCTURE

Just as the Unity synod offers guidance and direction to the various provinces of the Moravian Church, and as provincial (or district) synods have general supervision over local congregations, so an annual church council or congregational meeting guides and directs the individual churches. Annually, reports of the past year are presented; a budget adopted; and elders, trustees, and other officers are elected. Additional meetings of the council may be held as needed.

Between council meetings, of course, the elders and trustees are in charge of the life of the congregation. In some congregations the functions of the two boards are combined into a single church board. This parallels the executive function of provincial elders for the provinces and district executive boards for the districts.

The pastor is always chairperson of the elders; may be given place in trustees' meetings; and is in general charge of the life of the church, as enabler but not as dictator. Normally a local Moravian church is a democratic institution, where the name "Unity of Brothers and Sisters" is exemplified.

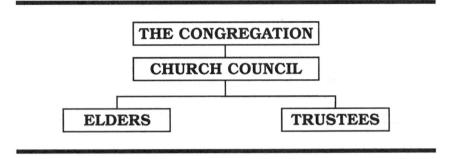

EXPECTATIONS

Over the years we all find that church membership is most satisfying and fruitful when the church meets members' expectations after they join, and the new members also meet the congregation's expectations. Naturally there are variations on both sides, but here is a summary of what a Moravian church usually expects. The big word is "commitment" and might well precede each item:

- Regular participation in worship.
- Financial support of the congregation and broader church, according to one's ability: if possible, a tithe.
- Serving when elected to a board or committee.
- Participation in the total church — the body of Christ.
- Giving witness (including evangelism) to God's love for the whole world, thus willingly offering service in the larger community where one lives.

Much has already been said about Moravians' concept of the church, but here is a kind of summary, again from "Essential Features of the Unity":

A LIVING CHURCH
The church is and remains a living one when it:
- *is attentive to God's word;*
- *confesses its sins and accepts forgiveness for them;*
- *seeks and maintains fellowship with its Lord and Redeemer by means of the sacraments;*

- *places its whole life under God's rule and daily leading;*
- *ministers to its neighbor and seeks fellowship with all who confess Christ;*
- *proclaims to the world the tidings concerning the Savior;*
- *awaits wholeheartedly the coming of its Lord as King.*

FUTURE OUTLOOK

Christians are at their best when they look to the future in faith and hope. The twenty-first century finds the church meeting new challenges bravely and wisely. After five and one half centuries of history, the Unitas Fratrum is apt to discover its future as a projection of its past.

MORAVIANS TODAY

MOTTO AND SEAL

Most institutions in modern society try to express their special characteristics or trademark in a logo or brief slogan. For the Moravian Church a phrase comes closest to this, although never made official: "In essentials, unity; in non-essentials, liberty; and in all things, love."

The motto is attributed to Bishop John Amos Comenius, and is surely as old as his time. For most Moravians the words apply only to doctrine. During all its long history, the Unitas Fratrum has not been a confessional church. It has at least half a dozen basic beliefs (see chapter 3) that it considers essential, but it tries to avoid binding its members to fine shades of doctrinal interpretation in a written creed.

This means that it will be an international church. It will be an ecumenical church. It will be a church leaning heavily on Scripture for authority and on Christ as its Head, yet ready to break new ground in order to serve well the new ages. It will continue to use strong personal ties to overcome conflict and to identify gifts for service.

Count Zinzendorf and the early Herrnhut community felt they had a special relationship to Jesus Christ, even as the ancient Hebrews believed they were in a covenant relationship with Yahweh. Moravians today still celebrate September 16 (a ministers' covenant day) and November 13 (a time for congregational Holy Communion) in recognition of Christ's headship over the church. The covenant relationship is regarded as the privilege of all Christians, not just Moravians.

One example is baptism. Ordinarily infants or adults are baptized in the Moravian Church by sprinkling or pouring the water. Immersion is not considered as essential. At the same time, if a member wishes to express faith through being immersed, this is quite acceptable.

The central point to the Moravians is this: Do the parents of the child, or the adult candidate, understand what God expects of the individuals who are party to baptism? Is cleansing from sin recognized as a human need? Is there faith that God through Christ can give new and whole life?

The seal of the Moravian Church goes back to the sixteenth century, possibly earlier. In the center of the seal is the Lamb of God, a favorite symbol of the early Christian church. A lamb is holding a staff, and from the staff waves a banner of victory. On the banner a cross is clearly displayed.

The uniqueness of the lamb symbol for Moravians is the inscription attached (often in a circular band): Vicit agnus noster, eum sequamur, "Our Lamb has conquered, let us follow him." It is found on church publications, in stained glass windows of churches, and among other appointments.

Compared to the Methodists and Baptists in America, the Moravians are numerically small. This is even true as compared to the Presbyterians or Lutherans, and scores of others. This does not bother most members of the denomination. The more basic question is, "Are Moravians serving the Lord Jesus Christ in fulfillment of their heritage?" And how can a group of 40,000 adults and children function as a national church in either the United States or Canada in the face of current mobility and dispersion?

IDENTITY

The Moravian identity must be clarified and consistently pursued, so that some sort of nationwide characteristics will stand out. Moravians are generally classified as bridge-building Protestants. They have things in common with most other churches and they identify few barriers to sharing life and ministry with other Christian churches. This does not mean the denomination cannot bear its own stamp and characteristics. One North Carolina pastor has put it this way:

> *At times we have tried to be all things to all people doctrinally speaking, emphasizing personal freedom and a religion of the heart. Without forfeiting such a valuable emphasis, and certainly without embracing a narrow dogmatism, we must articulate what we do believe and what doctrines and practices are not consistent with our understanding. The theological excesses of our day — for example, militant fundamentalism and electronic triumphalism — demand that we address theological issues.*

ENTHUSIASM

Another important ingredient of Moravian identity is enthusiasm. A Catholic historian, Ronald Knox, included the early American Moravians in his important book *Enthusiasm — A Chapter in the History of Religion.* A new burst of enthusiastic outreach, therefore, would be an extension of the Moravian heritage. A layman active in an urban, racially integrated Moravian church once said, "This place turns me on." A typical visitor to a Minnesota Moravian church was quoted by the pastor in these words:

There was also a sense of something important happening in your service. It wasn't deadly solemn like another church I visited, where it seemed as if they were just going through the motions, saying the right words and reciting the right prayers. I felt as if you were excited to be there and expected good things to happen.

In Ohio a visitor came to a new Moravian congregation and found this:

The small congregation was led by an enthusiastic, balding man whose energy was twice that of men half his age. His infectious enthusiasm brought us back week after week as he dealt with important spiritual issues and Christian growth from a biblical perspective that was practical and attractive.

We have remained with the church since that first visit. Its loving attitude, support, and atmosphere have caused me to consider my relationship with Christ more realistically than ever before.

ATMOSPHERE AND ACTION

The word *atmosphere* used in the previous statement draws attention to another quality in which Moravians should aim to excel. While it is urgent for all small churches to try to grow, thus fulfilling Christ's command to spread the gospel, even while small they can specialize in demonstrating that they care deeply about others. Visitors can tell, as soon as they enter a church door, whether the members are too involved in talking just among themselves or want to reach out warmly to others.

An *atmosphere* that reaches out warmly is one that welcomes questions, considers new ideas, and values flexibility. The newcomer soon discovers that underneath this accepting Moravian spirit is a faith grounded in Jesus Christ as Lord and in the "sole standard" of Scripture. As we have more and more contact with persons of different cultures, values, and religions, the atmosphere of both acceptance and conviction is increasingly important.

The right *atmosphere* in a congregation always leads to *action*. Undoubtedly beautiful customs will continue to cause Moravian churches to be crowded every Christmas and Easter, but worship in the "sanctuary" needs to find expression in ministry that serves the real needs of real people.

The internet and a myriad of new electronic devices are changing the ways people communicate and relate to each other. As Moravians continue to communicate the gospel of Jesus Christ and build relationships among his people, they must use the tools and methods of a new century.

Recently we had occasion to review a chapter in the history of one of the early Moravian settlements in the United States. Amazingly we found that Bishop August Spangenberg in that era had a 16-point plan of action! When nothing is planned, usually nothing happens.

CONCLUSION

A prominent United States church leader has referred to the Moravian Church as a "both-and" church. He articulated something very important to Moravians. They can enthusiastically devote themselves both to social justice and to personal evangelism. They can join "mainline" denominations in councils of churches and they can engage in conversation and action with evangelicals and Pentecostals. They can be both liturgical and free in worship. They can recognize accountability to a province and a Unity, even while they develop unique styles in local congregations. They look both inward in fellowship and mutual concern and outward in witness and service.

A continuing growth in numbers of Moravians in the Third World seems assured. More importantly, there is evidence of a deepening commitment to mission outreach across the entire church. And the Unity truly is a "unity." The Moravian faith is alive!

ℋISTORICAL NOTES

Organization dates of congregations in the United States and Canada
and dates of the worldwide Moravian Church:

JANUARY

1 - 1815	Sharon, Tuscarawas, Ohio
1858	Chaska, Minnesota
1915	Waconia, Minnesota
1968	United, New York, New York, merger of New York III and IV
3 - 1856	Ordination of John Andrew Buckley, the first Moravian minister of African descent, Antigua, West Indies
1932	First service of confirmation of Moravians in Honduras
5 - 1992	New Hope, Miami, Florida
12 - 1757	The first Moravian convert baptized on Antigua, West Indies
19 - 1964	Rio Terrace, Edmonton, Alberta, Canada
20 - 1889	Wisconsin Rapids, Wisconsin
21 - 1951	Konnoak Hills, Winston-Salem, North Carolina
28 - 1966	Palm Beach, West Palm Beach, Florida
30 - 1864	Sturgeon Bay, Wisconsin
31 - 1971	St. Paul's, Upper Marlboro, Maryland

FEBRUARY

2 - 1891	Bethel, Leonard, North Dakota
1964	Trinity, New Carrollton, Maryland
3 - 1957	Official organization of Morongo Moravian Church, Banning, California; result of Indian mission work begun in 1889
9 - 1749	Warwick, now Lititz, Lititz, Pennsylvania
12 - 1978	Covenant, Wilmington, North Carolina
1989	Good Shepherd, Kernersville, North Carolina
13 - 1870	Unionville, Michigan
1983	New Hope, Newton, North Carolina

MARCH

1 - 1457	Date observed in commemoration of the founding in Bohemia of the Unitas Fratrum, now known as the Moravian Church
5 - 1939	Calvary, Allentown, Pennsylvania

MARCH (continued)

14 - 1849	Arrival of first Moravian missionaries in Bluefields, Nicaragua
	1886	Great Kills, Staten Island, New York
14 - 1951	Mountainview, Hellertown, Pennsylvania
15 - 1925	Grace, Mount Airy, North Carolina
21 - 1993	King of Kings, Miami, Florida
23 - 1975	First, Stone Mountain, Georgia
24 - 1799	The first Moravian converts baptized on Tobago, West Indies
25 - 1752	First, York, Pennsylvania
27 - 1966	John Hus, Brooklyn, New York
28 - 1954	Lakeview, Madison, Wisconsin

APRIL

1 - 1756	Arrival on Antigua, West Indies, of Samuel Isles, the first Moravian missionary on that island
	1888	First, Easton, Pennsylvania
3 - 1896	Sister Bay, Wisconsin
4 - 1773	Friedberg, Winston-Salem, North Carolina
6 - 1851	Olivet, Winston-Salem, North Carolina
7 - 1929	Glenwood, Madison, Wisconsin
9 - 1917	Veedum, Pittsville, Wisconsin
10 - 1949	Palmer Township, Easton, Pennsylvania
	1988	Good News, Sherwood Park, Alberta, Canada
11 - 1898	Enterprise, Arcadia, North Carolina
13- 1732	The first Easter sunrise service of the Moravians conducted in the Hutberg cemetery at Herrnhut, Germany
	1760	Bethania, North Carolina
	1859	Egg Harbor City, New Jersey
	1885	Windsor, now Christian Faith, DeForest, Wisconsin
21 - 1929	Leaksville, Eden, North Carolina
	1976	Our Savior's, Altura, Minnesota, merger of Bethany and Hebron
25 - 1890	Arrival on Trinidad, West Indies, of Samuel Thaeler and John Holmes to organize Moravian work on that island
27 - 1790	Arrival on Tobago, West Indies, of John and Mary Montgomery (parents of hymnwriter James Montgomery) to begin Moravian work on that island
	1852	New York II, now Tremont Terrace, Bronx, New York
	1969	Christ, Calgary, Alberta, Canada

MAY

3 - 1728	Beginning of Losungen (Daily Texts) in Herrnhut, Germany
	1931	Rural Hall, North Carolina
5 - 1822	St. Philip's, Winston-Salem, North Carolina
	1895	Fairview, Winston-Salem, North Carolina

MAY (continued)

6 - 1860	West Side, Bethlehem, Pennsylvania
1895	Bruderheim, Alberta, Canada
12 - 1727	Unanimous adoption of the first statutes, or Brotherly Agreement, by the settlers at Herrnhut, Germany, the first definite step toward reorganization of the Unitas Fratrum
17 - 1863	Palmyra, Cinnaminson, New Jersey
18 - 1902	Calgary, now Good Shepherd, Calgary, Alberta, Canada
19 - 2002	New Beginnings, Huntersville, North Carolina
22 - 1966	Redeemer, Philadelphia, Pennsylvania
1983	Christ's Community Church, Maple Grove, Minnesota
24 - 1856	Macedonia, Advance, North Carolina
1878	Goshen, Durbin, North Dakota
25 - 1844	West Salem, Illinois
1986	Faith Church of the Nation's Capital, Washington, D.C.
26 - 1853	Ephraim, Wisconsin
1963	Acceptance of Saratoga Union, Wisconsin Rapids, Wisconsin, as a Moravian congregation

JUNE

1 - 1895	Rudolph, Wisconsin
5 - 1898	Willow Hill, Ararat, Virginia
6 - 1954	Downey, California
9 - 1957	East Hills, Bethlehem, Pennsylvania
11 - 1857	Fry's Valley, New Philadelphia, Ohio
12 - 1905	Edmonton, Alberta, Canada
1943	Fargo, now Shepherd of the Prairie, Fargo, North Dakota
1955	Battle Hill, Union, New Jersey, continuing the Elizabeth, New Jersey, congregation begun in 1866
14 - 1777	Arrival of the first Moravian missionaries on St. Kitts, West Indies
17 - 1722	Beginning of the building of Herrnhut, Germany, by the emigrants from Moravia
1830	Hope, Indiana
1853	Ebenezer, Watertown, Wisconsin
18 - 1932	Hopewell, Winston-Salem, North Carolina
20 - 1884	Arrival of first Moravian missionaries in Bethel, Alaska
21 - 1621	The Day of Blood, so called because on that day 27 patriots, most of them members of the Brethren's Church, were executed at Prague, Bohemia
1924	Advent, Winston-Salem, North Carolina
1958	Grace, Westland, Michigan
25 - 1742	Central, Bethlehem, Pennsylvania
1747	Nazareth, Pennsylvania
1876	Fries Memorial, Winston-Salem, North Carolina

JUNE (continued)

26 - 1988   Fellowship, Brooklyn, New York
27 - 1895   Bruderfeld, now Millwoods, Edmonton, Alberta, Canada
29 - 1924   Ardmore, Winston-Salem, North Carolina

JULY

6 - 1415   Burning at the stake of John Hus, Bohemian martyr
and forebear of the Unitas Fratrum
1763   New Dorp, Staten Island, New York
1800   Gnadenhutten, Ohio
14 - 1912   Trinity, Winston-Salem, North Carolina
17 - 1955   Grace, Center Valley, Pennsylvania
1927   Crooked Oak, Cana, Virginia
26 - 1846   New Philadelphia, Winston-Salem, North Carolina
1896   Heimtal, South Edmonton, Alberta, Canada
30 - 1747   Emmaus, Pennsylvania
31 - 1752   Arrival of first Moravian missionaries in Labrador

AUGUST

13 - 1727   Manifestation of the unity of the Spirit, at the Holy
Communion service held in the Berthelsdorf, Germany,
church; regarded as the spiritual birthday of the Renewed
Moravian Church
1837   Newfoundland, Pennsylvania
1900   Clemmons, North Carolina
21 - 1732   Departure of the first Moravian missionaries from Herrnhut
for St. Thomas in the West Indies; the beginning of Moravian
missions and of the modern missionary movement of the
Protestant church
26 - 1780   Hope, Winston-Salem, North Carolina
2001   The Promise, Lewis Center, Ohio
27 - 1727   Beginning of the Hourly Intercession
1872   Formation of the Moravian Prayer Union
31 - 1873   Castleton Hill, Staten Island, New York

SEPTEMBER

3 - 1780   Friedland, Winston-Salem, North Carolina
5 - 1869   Northfield, Minnesota
10 - 1911   Daggett, Michigan
11 - 1854   Watertown, Wisconsin
13 - 1893   Union Cross, Winston-Salem, North Carolina
1896   Mizpah, Rural Hall, North Carolina
15 - 2003   Holly Springs, North Carolina

SEPTEMBER (continued)

16 - 1741	Recognition and acceptance of Christ as the Chief Elder of the Moravian Church
1858	Canadensis, Pennsylvania
1984	New Dawn, Toronto, Ontario, Canada
18 - 1768	Baptism of the first Moravian convert on Barbados, West Indies
25 - 1887	Oak Grove, Winston-Salem, North Carolina
26 - 1765	Arrival of John Wood and Andrew Rittsmansberger on Barbados, West Indies, from Herrnhut to begin Moravian work

OCTOBER

2 - 1807	Beginning of the Moravian Theological Seminary at Nazareth, Pennsylvania, in 1858 transferred to Bethlehem
3 - 1762	Schoeneck, Nazareth, Pennsylvania
1896	Moravia, Summerfield, North Carolina
4 - 1953	Raleigh, North Carolina
5 - 1908	First, Greensboro, North Carolina
1924	King, North Carolina
6 - 1889	London, Cambridge, Wisconsin
7 - 2002	Immanuel-New Eden, merger of Immanuel (1912) and New Eden (1923)
8 - 1758	Graceham, Thurmont, Maryland
1967	Rolling Hills, Longwood, Florida
10 - 1885	Moving into the first house in Bethel, Alaska, by missionaries John Kilbuck and William Weinland
12 - 1851	East Side, Green Bay, Wisconsin
17 - 2004	Cordero de Dios, Winston-Salem, North Carolina
18 - 1889	Stapleton, now Vanderbilt Avenue, Staten Island, New York
20 - 1985	Church of the Redeemer, Dublin, Ohio
22 - 1899	Bethesda, Winston-Salem, North Carolina
23 - 1881	Canaan, Davenport, North Dakota
24 - 1874	First, Uhrichsville, Ohio
25 - 1896	Christ, Winston-Salem, North Carolina
1914	Edgeboro, Bethlehem, Pennsylvania
31 - 1858	Lake Auburn, Victoria, Minnesota

NOVEMBER

7 - 1920	The Little Church on the Lane, Charlotte, North Carolina
9 - 1980	Grace, Queens, New York
10 - 1867	Kernersville, North Carolina
11 - 1893	Fulp, Walnut Cove, North Carolina
12 - 1909	Kellner, Wisconsin Rapids, Wisconsin

NOVEMBER (continued)

13 - 1741	Formal announcement to the congregations of the Moravian Church of the immediate Headship of the Lord Jesus Christ in his church on earth
1771	Home, Winston-Salem, North Carolina
1893	Calvary, Winston-Salem, North Carolina
1965	Covenant, York, Pennsylvania, merger of Bethany and Olivet
14 - 1779	Baptism of the first Moravian convert on St. Kitts, West Indies
16 - 1924	Pine Chapel, Winston-Salem, North Carolina
1980	Unity, Lewisville, North Carolina
17 - 1753	Arrival of the first Moravians from Bethlehem, Pennsylvania, on the Wachovia Tract in North Carolina to establish a settlement; observed as the anniversary of Bethabara, the first congregation of the Southern Province
1850	Fort Howard, now West Side, Green Bay, Wisconsin
18 - 1930	Beginning of Moravian work in Honduras by George Heath in Cauquira
1951	Messiah, Winston-Salem, North Carolina
21 - 1880	Providence, Winston-Salem, North Carolina
24 - 1963	Park Road, Charlotte, North Carolina, name Peace adopted in 1999
1991	Christ the King, Durham, North Carolina
25 - 1852	Mt. Bethel, Cana, Virginia
29 - 1896	Mayodan, North Carolina
30 - 1746	Lancaster, Pennsylvania
1986	Prince of Peace, Miami, Florida

DECEMBER

4 - 1874	Berea, St. Charles, Minnesota
9 - 1883	Coopersburg, Pennsylvania
11 - 1887	College Hill, Bethlehem, Pennsylvania
13 - 1732	Arrival of Leonard Dober and David Nitschmann, the first foreign missionaries of the Moravian Church, on St. Thomas, West Indies
16 - 1877	Fries Memorial, Winston-Salem, North Carolina
17 - 1914	Reading, Pennsylvania
19 - 1747	Lebanon, Pennsylvania
21 - 1856	Lake Mills, Wisconsin
22 - 1866	Freedom, Appleton, Wisconsin
25 - 1862	First, South Bethlehem, Pennsylvania, now Advent, Bethlehem, Pennsylvania
27 - 1748	First, New York, New York
1842	First, Dover, Ohio
31 - 1865	First, Riverside, New Jersey
1947	Schoenbrunn, New Philadelphia, Ohio